# Online Interviewing

# Online Interviewing

## Nalita James and Hugh Busher

Los Angeles | London | New Delhi
Singapore | Washington DC

SAGE Publications Ltd
1 Oliver's Yard
55 City Road
London EC1Y 1SP

SAGE Publications Inc.
2455 Teller Road
Thousand Oaks, California 91320

SAGE Publications India Pvt Ltd
B 1/I 1 Mohan Cooperative Industrial Area
Mathura Road, New Delhi 110 044
India

SAGE Publications Asia-Pacific Pte Ltd
33 Pekin Street #02-01
Far East Square
Singapore 048763

**Library of Congress Control Number 2008943692**

**British Library Cataloguing in Publication data**

A catalogue record for this book is available
from the British Library

ISBN 978-1-4129-4531-8
ISBN 978-1-4129-4532-5 (pbk)

Typeset by C&M Digitals (P) Ltd, Chennai, India
Printed in the UK by the MPG Books Group
Printed on paper from sustainable resources

# Contents

# About the Authors

**Dr Nalita James** is lecturer in Employment Studies in the Centre for Labour Market Studies, University of Leicester. Her methodological research interests in the use of the Internet in qualitative research stemmed from her doctoral research that examined academics' workplace learning and communities of practice using email interviews. She has recently published in this area in the *International Journal of Research and Method in Education and Qualitative Research* (with Hugh Busher) and the *British Educational Research Journal*. She is currently developing research with Hugh Busher to further explore the methodological capacities of the Internet. She is also currently researching and writing about the impact of creativity on young adults' learning transitions as well as creative professionals' workplace learning.

**Dr Hugh Busher** is a senior lecturer in the School of Education, University of Leicester. He was, until 2005, Coordinator of a British Educational Research Association (BERA) Special Interest Group (SIG) on Leading and Managing Schools and Colleges and a member of BERA Council. He was until recently co-editor of the journal *Improving Schools* published by SAGE Publications. He has had extensive experience of teaching in secondary schools and in universities. Long-standing areas of research interest focus on critical perspectives on the processes of schools and other educational organisations:

- students and the construction of equity, values and social justice in education;
- leadership, power and change processes in educational organisations, especially schools;
- the construction of professional development and identity by teachers and other staff in schools;
- the interaction of policy and community contexts with the micro-political processes of teaching, learning and decision-making in schools.

He has been involved in a number of research projects since 2000. These focused on the work of support staff and teachers in secondary schools; on the construction by teachers of their professional identities and practice; and on the impact of teachers' activities (and the educational values and pedagogic views these reflect) on other staff and on students. The projects include: Evaluating IQEA in Nottinghamshire, Nottinghamshire County Council,

(2002); Being and Becoming Middle Leaders in Secondary Schools: How Some Middle Leaders in Secondary Schools Construct Their Work Related Identities and Influence Decision-making (2002–3); Case studies in Inclusion and Engagement in Schools in Beirut (2005–7). His most recent book was *Understanding Educational Leadership: People, Power and Culture* (Open University Press, 2006).

# Acknowledgements

To some extent, this book began back in 1998 when Nalita commenced her doctoral research, which examined academics' workplace learning and communities of practice. Her participants were geographically dispersed and she could not afford the travel costs to visit them onsite at the various higher education institutions they were located at. At the same time she came across a journal article by Selwyn and Robson (1998) about the Internet and email interviewing and she realised that this virtual arena could offer exciting possibilities for her research design. So, she would like to thank Selwyn and Robson, *and* all the participants who took part in the email interviews. They invested time and commitment to those interviews and provided some rich and insightful reflections on the process of engaging in online research, and many of their comments are included in this book.

About the same time, Hugh was becoming interested in the possibilities of involving his many doctoral students in research about their experiences of trying to negotiate entry to the academy, building on the work of Bourdieu, Passeron and St Martin (1994). Unlike the French researchers' students who were all conveniently located in one accessible place in Paris, his were scattered throughout Europe and the Middle East, mainly in Lebanon. Their willingness to engage in playing with online interviewing to learn about a potential new approach to qualitative research methods opened a lot of windows from which this book, in part, arose.

So this book is a joint venture and we would like to acknowledge the invaluable support of the other in bringing it to fruition. In an interestingly postmodern way, without the creativity of the other this text would probably not have emerged, at least in the form that it has. In writing this book we have had many interesting discussions about the virtual world and its epistemological, ethical and methodological possibilities and challenges. Such discussions have inspired us to continue to research and write about the Internet and online research.

Finally, we would like to thank Patrick Brindle for taking an interest in our work at the Sixth International Conference on Social Science held at the University of Amsterdam in 2004 and encouraging us to submit a book proposal, as well as providing invaluable support and advice about the construction of this book.

*Nalita James and Hugh Busher*

# Introduction

Online research methods are increasingly being taught on mainstream courses, particularly to Social Science students at masters and doctoral level. This often builds on the experiences of researchers who have used online research for quantitative surveys and questionnaires through tools such as email, websites and software packages. However researchers are now increasingly using the Internet as a vehicle for qualitative online research. In this they are adapting a range of familiar qualitative research methods tools, such as different types of interviews, to engage with participants across different time zones and places at times convenient to them without the considerable costs involved in travelling. This innovative approach remains at present theoretically underdeveloped.

This book considers the merits and complexities of using these qualitative research tools to conduct online synchronous (real-time) interviews and asynchronous (non-real time) interviews. Central to this is the question of how researchers can construct trustworthy knowledge that is of benefit to the readers of it. It leads to the consideration not only of epistemology – the construction and verification of knowledge through the means by which it is collected and analysed – but also to how that knowledge can be collected ethically. As in all qualitative research a key element is the relationships that researchers build up with their willing participants.

The authors examine critically the ethical, methodological and epistemological challenges that face researchers who carry out different types of online qualitative synchronous and asynchronous interviews. They do this by:

- Reviewing the epistemological issues surrounding online qualitative research, with specific focus on different approaches to online interviewing.
- Examining the methodological complexities involved in designing and conducting online interviews in qualitative research. Their value as a research tool is also considered in the light of both the similarities and differences compared with onsite interviews.
- Considering the ethical implications of, and the flows of, inequalities and power that occur in online interviewing.
- Exploring the theoretical and epistemological challenges surrounding the collection and analysis of data in online interviews.

To achieve these aims the book draws on our own research as well as a broad range of international research studies that have used online qualitative interviewing to show researchers the methodological and theoretical considerations associated with this approach, supported by vignettes of practice to illustrate these. We too, are active qualitative researchers who have acquired our Internet expertise through our involvement in two separate studies using email interviewing to understand the narratives through which our participants expressed their perspectives of their work experiences and identities.

The discussions throughout this book are intended to stimulate ongoing debate about these research approaches, particularly when compared with onsite qualitative interviews. By onsite the authors refer to those methods which are not conducted in the virtual environment but in particular face-to-face interviews. Through this examination, the authors highlight the need for researchers to consider a range of methodological issues before deciding whether online qualitative interviews are appropriate for the topics they want to investigate.

It is anticipated that the book will be suitable as both a core and supplementary text for those undertaking research methods courses across the social sciences at postgraduate level. Although the text is primarily designed for this, it is also expected to appeal to professional researchers who need to understand the methodological and epistemological challenges of carrying out online interviews in the virtual environment, as well as the new ethical issues that researchers are faced with. So it assumes that readers will have some familiarity with many of the issues associated with qualitative interviewing.

The book provides a well-reasoned introduction to the challenges of online qualitative research especially as enacted through different types of interviews. It is not intended as a 'how to do it book' but it does offer researchers a variety of practical advice in each chapter. However, it is intended to encourage researchers to engage with the critical, practical and theoretical issues that must be considered in the conduct of online qualitative interviews

The book is structured into 10 chapters each dealing with different ethical, methodological and practical issues surrounding the conduct of online qualitative research. Chapter 1 introduces the aims of the book. In doing so, it explores how the advent of the Internet has inspired new ways of thinking about the nature of qualitative inquiry and how research is conducted using different methods of data collection. It takes up the theoretical concerns about how knowledge is constructed in qualitative research and the potential this holds for online interviewing.

Chapter 2 examines how knowledge is constructed and accessed in online environments. It investigates the nature of online relationships and communication, in both naturalistic and constructed research settings. It examines different approaches to online communication in terms of asynchronicity and synchronicity and the nature of interactions that emerge (reflexive and spontaneous) between researcher and participant. It discusses the implications this has for collecting online interview data as researchers try to make sense of their participants' social worlds and sustain meaningful research relationships with them online.

Chapter 3 examines qualitative methodologies and methods that have used online communications as a platform from which collecting data from individuals. It also considers the opportunities for developing and understanding online research practices. This includes discussion of the conduct of virtual ethnographies. It considers the value of combining online/virtual and offline/real interactions with research participants, and the methodological implications this has for online research.

Chapter 4 looks at the impact of the displacement of time and space in online research, especially through interviewing, and the implications this has for research participants. It considers how knowledge is constructed in a disembodied, anonymous and textual environment. It discusses how such an environment affects research relationships when visual and verbal cues are absent. It also examines approaches to interviewing when conducting them asynchronously and in real-time.

Chapter 5 examines a range of ethical issues that confront the qualitative online researcher. It considers how ethical principles associated with onsite interviews can be transfered to qualitative online research, especially when collecting sensitive and personal information. The main issues are the construction of informed consent in order for researchers to gain ethical access to research sites, the construction of trustworthy data and the protection of participants from harm by guaranteeing the confidentiality, privacy and security of their data. The last is bound up with the complexities of delineating public and private online spaces. An element of this is the application of netiquette. It is not possible to consider such issues without discussing the impact of cross-cultural studies on the ethics of research.

Chapter 6 explores the credibility and authenticity of data when gathered using online interviews. It discusses the implications of textual self-presentation for assuring the authenticity of research projects, and what leads researchers to accept participants' statements of identity at face value when they lack the information provided in face-to-face encounters. It also examines the debates around combining online and offline research and whether by doing so, it is possible to get closer to social reality as a means of enhancing the rigour of the constructed method and the credibility of the data.

Chapter 7 examines the impact on research projects of the power relations and inequalities that exist between researchers and participants. In particular, it examines how, in the faceless context of the Internet, individuals assert and protect their agency and identity from positions of remoteness. This includes considering the impact of new technologies and the cultures associated with them on social processes, such as processes of work and the construction of people's identities and the cultural and political environments in which people work. The inherent inequalities of power in research projects have important implications for how researchers construct their online interviews, and the ways in which researchers have to approach and work with potential online participants in their studies.

Chapter 8 focuses on interrogating meanings in the third spaces of online qualitative research (both synchronous and asynchronous interviews). It begins by considering how such spaces lead to the negotiation of cultural hybridity and the construction of small cultures by researchers and other participants engaged in the text/speech acts of online exchanges. In turn this leads, first, to consideration of the nature of the cultures of online research communities. Second, it leads to a discussion of the analysis of online discourses that are constructed in these disembodied third spaces.

Chapter 9 considers the contradiction of gathering public data for socially beneficially research while protecting the private lives of project participants. It considers general frameworks for curating data which shape how online researchers organise, store, analyse and distribute qualitative interview data. It also examines how issues related to the publication and dissemination of research outcomes contribute to the dilemmas in deciding what is public and private data when research is conducted online.

Chapter 10 draws together the book and reflects on the many challenges and possibilities that the Internet presents to researchers when they attempt to carry out online interviews for research purposes. In particular it considers the practical implications raised, and how researchers can surmount the epistemological and methodological challenges and opportunities that face them in constructing online research methods, such as interviews. It discusses how online researchers can cope with the ethical and political processes that surround them, and how they can surmount the cultural and personal conundrums of creating trustworthy online conversations. The chapter concludes by considering how to construct collaborative online research cultures that will facilitate participants' engagement in online research projects or research projects that use online methods.

From the above discussion, it is evident that researchers using the Internet to conduct online interviews face some serious epistemological, methodological and ethical questions in their research practice. The online setting does differ from the face-to-face and this has important implications for the research process in terms of time and space constraints, modes of communication supported, and a blurred distinction between public and private domains. Together, with our and other studies discussed in this book, we hope our experiences will offer an invaluable basis for extending discussion, debate and innovation about such issues, in the conduct of Internet-based online interviews.

A companion website for this book can be found at the following URL: http://www. sagepub.co.uk/jamesandbusher/

# ONE

# Epistemological Dimensions in Qualitative Research: the Construction of Knowledge Online

Overview: this chapter introduces the aims of the book. In doing so, it explores how the advent of the Internet has inspired new ways of thinking about the nature of qualitative inquiry and how research is conducted using different methods of data collection. It takes up the theoretical concerns about how knowledge is constructed in qualitative research and the potential this holds for online interviewing.

## Introduction

In a matter of very few years, the Internet has consolidated itself as a powerful platform that has changed the way individuals communicate. In 2007, there were 1.24 billion Internet users (Burkeman, 2008). The Internet has become the universal source of information for millions of people, at home, at school and at work. It has had significant impact on the conditions of social interaction and the way in which individuals construct the reality of everyday lives. It has reconfigured the way in which individuals communicate and connect with each other. The 'trajectory of acquaintanceship development' has become such that individuals can now first get to know each other online through chat rooms, before using other media such as email, telephone and face-to-face contact (Zhao, 2006: 471). There has been a rapid increase in websites such as YouTube, MySpace, Facebook and blogs of many descriptions, that allow people to present themselves, create presentations of themselves, present their views and invite the views of others. Such websites also offer opportunities for 'social networking' and they are clearly reshaping the way in which news and views are gathered and disseminated (Goodfellow, 2007).

Coinciding with the global expansion of the Internet, is its popularisation as a research medium for the collection of primary data, as seen in marketing research and the field of communications and media research. More recently, the Internet has been used as a research medium in the social sciences, opening up innovative ways for researchers to examine human inter/actions and experiences in new contexts. Consequently, there has been a growth of literature discussing the Internet as a tool for research. Over the last decade there has been a number of ground-breaking books including Jones (1999) *Doing Internet Research*, an edited collection of studies which examined Internet research methods, Mann and Stewart (2000) *Internet Communication and Qualitative Research* and Hine (2000) *Virtual Ethnography*. These texts have examined the impact of Internet technology as both a medium for collecting data, and a product of culture that infiltrates other spaces and times of its participants. Further, virtual training packages such as that developed by Madge et al. (2006) have been critical in enhancing users' understanding of both qualitative and quantitative online research methods.

Advances in Internet technology have offered researchers innovative approaches to online research in the social sciences (Jankowski and van Selm, 2005). The Internet has had considerable affect on the way in which qualitative inquiry takes place in the social sciences. In particular, it has altered the nature of context in which research takes place, and knowledge is constructed. 'Electronic virtuality is now embedded within actuality in a more dispersed and active way than ever before' (Hammersley, 2006: 8).

The Internet has offered researchers exciting possibilities to explore and understand human experience by taking conventional research designs and methods and adapting them for the virtual environment. Hine (2005: 5) has commented that: 'Research on the "Internet" is marked as a distinct topic worthy of specific note by the introduction of new epithets to familiar methods.' The Internet offers a different space and dimension in which familiar research methods can be used to allow researchers to write about who their participants are, and what they know. Further 'Each manifestation of these technologies of mediation presents opportunities for the evolution of those traditional methods of social investigation' (Stewart and Williams, 2005: 396).

The Internet has greatly expanded the possibilities of conducting research with individuals and communities, providing a virtual social arena where practices, meanings and identities can intermingle between researchers and participants in ways that may not be possible in the real world (Dominguez et al., 2007). This raises questions around how researchers:

(i) Enter the virtual world to collect and communicate participants' experiences.
(ii) Understand experience, and explain how they know what they know in the virtual world.
(iii) Ensure that such knowledge is adequate and legitimate, given the social, cultural and legal terrain of the Internet.

This book examines such issues by focusing on the use of interviewing as an online method of qualitative inquiry. The online interview presents both methodological and ethical potential and versatility in social science research. It also presents methodological and ethical challenges that need to be addressed when using the Internet to conduct research.

## Constructing Knowledge in Qualitative Inquiry

Qualitative research recognises the importance of value and context, setting and the participants' frames of reference. Further, the way in which the researcher and participant enter and communicate the research field is a vital and influential element of the research process and its outcomes. Research that is conducted using qualitative methods acknowledges the existence and study of the interplay of multiple views and voice. It also allows for the construction of reality and knowledge to be mapped out. Yet, this knowledge cannot be understood without understanding the meaning that individuals attribute to that knowledge – their thoughts, feelings beliefs and actions (Illingworth, 2006). The construction of knowledge in qualitative research is related to the philosophical underpinnings that researchers choose whether the methods of data collection in that research are used on site or in an online site.

In trying to make sense of social reality, no grand method or theory has a universal and general claim to authoritative knowledge (Richardson, 1997: 121). Researchers engage in the practical activities of generating and interpreting data to answer questions about the meaning of what their participants know and do. They can do this using a wide range of methods including ethnography, life history work and narrative inquiry to study '... *first hand* what people do and say in particular contexts' (Hammersley, 2006: 4). To do this, researchers' practice will be underpinned by epistemological stances that provide a philosophical grounding for deciding what kinds of knowledge are possible, and how researchers can ensure they are both adequate and legitimate (Maynard, 1994: 10). There is a range of epistemologies as briefly summarised in Table 1.1 that form the foundations of social research (Crotty, 1998) and highlight how knowledge can be generated. These stances are reflected in qualitative research methodologies and methods that researchers employ.

Table 1.1    Three epistemologies

| Objectivism | Constructivism | Subjectivism |
|---|---|---|
| Meaning and meaningful reality exists as such apart from the operation of any consciousness. In this epistemology, of what it means to know, understanding and values are considered objectified in the people researchers study. | Constructivism rejects the objectivist view of human knowledge. Truth or meaning is constructed not discovered. People may construct meaning in different ways, even in relation to the same phenomena. There can be no unmediated grasp of the social world that exists independently of the researcher and all claims to knowledge take place within a particular conceptual framework. | Evident in structuralist, post-structuralist and postmodernist thinking. Meaning does not emerge from the interaction between the object and the subject; it is imposed on the object by the subject. |

*Source*: Crotty (1998).

Table 1.2   Philosophical assumptions in the generation of knowledge in qualitative research

| Phenomenology | Hermeneutics | Symbolic interactionism |
|---|---|---|
| Human behaviour is a product of how individuals interpret the world. The aim is to grasp and understand how individuals come to interpret theirs and others actions meaningfully. It requires researchers to engage with phenomena and make sense of them directly and immediately. | Meaning is participative and thus cannot be produced by the researcher. The point is not to reveal truth but to engage with the effects of tradition in a dialogical encounter with what is not understood and clarify the conditions in which understanding may take place, and thus disclose meaning. | Interaction takes place in such a way that the individual continually interprets the symbolic meaning of his/her environment. Researchers catch the process of interpretation through which individuals construct their actions. |

*Source*: Crotty (1998).

Epistemology has considerable bearing on the way researchers undertake their research projects. Some researchers interested in the social world are critical of the objectivism found in positivist and post-positivist stances that apply the methods of the natural sciences to the study of social reality and beyond (see Bryman, 2004 for a more detailed discussion of objectivism). Instead, researchers have argued for the need to focus social inquiry on understanding subjective meanings and values of individual actions. Such a stance can be linked to Max Weber's (1864–1920) *Verstehen* (understanding). To find meaning in action, requires researchers to interpret in a particular way what individuals are doing (Schwandt, 2000: 191). This process of interpretation can be differently represented through hermeneutics, phenomenology and symbolic interactionism. These philosophical or theoretical positions embrace different perspectives on the aims of understanding human action, different ethical commitments, and methodological and epistemological issues (Schwandt, 2000: 190). These philosophies provide a lens through which researchers can examine the research process and data. The kind of lens researchers choose to work with will influence how they view and make sense of the social world as a researcher. Table 1.2 gives an overview of these philosophies that provide different ways of addressing what individuals are doing or saying. It can also be used to explain the aims and methods of qualitative inquiry.

There are parallels between these stances and each will have distinctive epistemological concerns for the qualitative researcher, and different ways of addressing those concerns. At the very least, researchers have to decide on what is or should be regarded as acceptable knowledge. In doing so they should consider:

(i) How to define what 'understanding' means and how to justify claims to understand.

(ii) How to conceive and frame the research project.

(iii) How to occupy the ethical space where researcher and participant relate to one another in a project. (Schwandt, 2000: 200)

As social scientists, understanding the contexts and actions in which people live out their lives is important for making sense of the discourses they construct. Qualitative research does not have to carry with it fixed epistemological implications. Researchers have to decide what knowledge they want to gather about the social world. However, epistemological assumptions, values and methods may be inextricably intertwined.

This also applies to research on the Internet where people's everyday multiple realities are spatial and temporal. Advocates of postmodernism see the Internet as a blurring of the distinction between the virtual and the real world. This has created both hyper-reality and hyper-identity, leading to a loss of distinctions and consequent sense of fragmentation (Maclure, 1995). The Internet has altered the realities of everyday lives in which individuals interact with each other. It has been substantially broadened to include '... social phenomena of massive time-space extension' (Giddens, 1984: 85). The advent of modernity has increasingly torn space away from place by 'fostering relations between "absent" others, locationally distant from any given situation of face-to-face interaction' (Giddens, 1990: 18–19). Online, participants can take on meaningful and multiple identities in ways never before possible, leading to fundamental shifts in how individuals create, experience and understand identity (Turkle, 1995). The Internet, then, can provide a way of ordering human activity in the social world (Cavanagh, 2007: 146). The emergence of email, instant messaging and chat rooms as well as online public domains has altered the possibilities, scope and general basis of knowledge. This has implications for the nature of reality and existence in the social world and the nature of relationships that exist between individuals and communities. To understand reality and being in the virtual world, researchers can now look at humans as they are online (Capurro and Pringle, 2002). It is now possible for individuals who have never met face-to-face to have intimate, mutual knowledge through frequent online interactions (Zhao, 2006: 465). Participants and researchers from distant locations and diverse cultural backgrounds can come to know each other too, and construct meanings without ever seeing each other (Bowker and Tuffin, 2004).

The Internet, despite the absence of face-to-face interactions, creates a setting for research purposes and provides considerable opportunities to study the world beyond reach from the point of view of individuals and groups (Lincoln and Guba, 2000). In naturalistic settings, such as virtual communities, researchers can gain knowledge about the meaning of action taking place.

This approach emphasises the aims of interpretive research to study 'participants' ideas, attitudes, motives and intentions, and the way they interpret the social world' (Foster, 2006: 61), whether or not participants are online. It can empower participants to engage in action as individuals, and as members of a virtual community. Further, a researcher can join participants in these communities to explore how they co-construct their world in the circumstances in which they find themselves. As researchers immerse themselves in virtual communities to discover insightful findings about participants' private lives and social worlds, conversations about these lives can be broadened and democratised, rather than simply becoming records of human experience.

Researchers can acquire, explain and understand their participants' online experiences through a dialogic and reflexive encounter. This can become part of the interpretive act itself and the ongoing development of participants' viewpoints during the telling of experience. This process can be enhanced by researchers embracing both temporal and contextual dimensions of individuals' experiences (Illingworth, 2006). Adopting this approach broadly reflects the hermeneutical position. It allows time and space to explore what is not understood as well as clarifying the conditions in which understanding has taken place, and thus discloses meaning. Through this process, the meaning of conversation and interaction can be negotiated mutually in the act of interpretation, rather than simply discovered. From this perspective participants and researchers work together to construct understandings of the situations in which participants are living and working. Participants become co-constructors of knowledge of the situations which they inhabit as well as interpreters of the knowledge about a situation that emerges during the course of a research project. Researchers can gain a richer understanding of the practices of cultural and social life by examining the interrelationship between people, places and practices (Rybas and Gajjala, 2007). It illustrates the significance of the context of communication, paying attention to 'where' and 'how' (Illingworth, 2006).

Embracing the hermeneutic stance means researchers not only try to understand the context of shared meanings or practices that shape actions, but individual perspectives of the situation being investigated. Social actions cannot be extracted from, nor exist independently of, their context. However, the meanings that researchers draw from such contexts does demand caution as to whether knowledge generated in one context will be applicable to others (Doherty, 2007: 5). The stance may then pose a number of challenges for online researchers. The meanings that participants and researchers bring to the shared context of online interactions may be affected by the connections of time and space which occur differently in face-to-face interactions. This means that researchers need to build a detailed account of the online context. In face-to-face qualitative research the physical, visual and embodied ways of knowing provide a legitimate means to identify and explain the epistemological stance that researchers adopt. When interviews are conducted online, these frames of reference are lost, leading to reliance on the written word. Whether online research is composed asynchronously or synchronously the construction of knowledge will occur through textual means of representation (Doherty, 2007: 6). Methodologically, researchers may need to consider other factors that can shape participants' perspectives such as biographies and identities.

Yet, the text-based temporal and spatial nature of virtual communication means that researchers can 'collect rich data about the subjective self, a self accessed in what may be experienced as an almost transparent process of relating to one's own consciousness' (Mann and Stewart, 2000: 95). This can lead to a 'textual reflexivity' that reveals the 'text as much more – and also much less – than just a transparent representation of "the way things are"' (Stones, 1996: 97). This can encourage participants to engage in a more expansive discussion, and give online researchers an insight into the frames that participants use to constitute their reality, and the complexities of human expression. However, from a social constructivist position, such texts are devoid of meaning in their own right. Meaning is a process that is socially determined. It cannot exist independently of the interpreter and so all claims to knowledge will occur in a particular conceptual framework. Knowing is not passive. Individuals make knowledge and make sense of it. Meaning is constructed through the world and objects in the world (Illingworth, 2006).

All these challenges (and opportunities) raise questions about the nature of research practice that is adopted by online researchers to capture such sources of knowledge. Some researchers have argued in favour of an epistemology and ontology of research that stresses 'the hybrid and unfinished character of cyberspace ...' (Teli et al., 2007). In other words, if researchers are to understand life online, they have to understand that participants' experiences are connected and shaped by cultural and social elements that are both real and virtual, public and private and online and offline. To capture this connectedness suggests a methodology that can research the connected spaces – the real-contexts and actions of the research participants and their exploits online.

## Methods of Data Collection in the Construction of Knowledge: Face-to-face and Online Interviewing

Knowledge in qualitative research is constructed through the social processes of researchers engaging with the other participants in their studies. Research using qualitative methods are closely linked to researchers' different visions of how social reality should be studied, and what can be regarded as acceptable knowledge (Bryman, 2004). In the construction of knowledge, social scientists have viewed the face-to-face encounter as the optimal way to actively engage with research participants in qualitative research (Seymour, 2001). It has been perceived as the most powerful way in which researchers can seek to gain an understanding of how people construct their lives and the stories they tell about them (Fontana and Frey, 2003). When researcher and participant(s) meet face-to-face, physical and visual interaction can provide detail on each others' identity and about the situation eliciting the emotion (Sade-Beck, 2004). The presence of verbal and non-verbal cues such as facial expressions, gestures, postures and emotional mannerisms all add a further layer to individuals' social presence, and to the social interaction taking place. In the exchange of such cues, researcher and participant(s) can observe each others' behaviours and attributes.

In these face-to-face encounters, researchers use a variety of research methods to study everyday life and social interactions, to reveal the rich symbolic world that underlies needs, desires, meanings and choice (see for example Oakley, 1981; Atkinson and Hammersley, 1998; Flick, 2002). Such methods are designed to develop 'an *analytic* understanding of individual's perspectives, activities and actions … that [are] likely to be different from, perhaps even in conflict with, how the people themselves see the world' (Hammersley, 2006: 4, original emphasis). Further, the use of multiple methods such as case studies, personal experience and stories and visual texts to describe moments and meanings in individual lives, allows researchers to collect rich, descriptive and contextually situated data in order to seek understandings of human experience or relationships within a community or culture (Silverman, 1999).

The use of qualitative interviews in the social sciences has led to a broad range of discussions about how such interviews are designed and used as a method of data collection, and where they are located epistemologically and methodologically. Atkinson and Silverman (1997) argue that this has created an 'interview society' in which there is, 'a commitment to and reliance on the interview to produce narrative experience …' (Fontana and Frey, 2003: 63). Interviews as social arenas provide both vehicles and sites through which people construct and contest explications for their views and actions (Foucault, 1977). These arenas can include both group and individual interviews that produce a wealth of data about people's experiences, thoughts and feelings from their perspective. These methods then can become the site for the construction, interpretation, understanding and representation of experience.

Constructing knowledge in online research takes many forms. To date, social scientists have explored how traditional qualitative methods of research can be utilised and adapted in the virtual arena to examine how they make and validate knowledge as well as what that knowledge is. Researchers can engage in one-to-one interviews or with participants in groups to investigate the social processes of existing online communities. For example, Bampton and Cowton (2002) used email to interview teachers about their experiences of teaching management accounting in higher education. Hinton-Smith (2006) also used email to explore the experiences of lone parents as HE students.

Addrianssens and Cadman (1999) set up an asynchronous focus group study to explore the launch of an online market share-trading platform in the UK, in which questions were emailed to the participants. Finally, O'Connor and Madge (2001) employed conferencing software in connection with a virtual synchronous focus group study on the use of online information for parents.

In their studies, these researchers were faced with the epistemological challenge of understanding human action and experience, as well as understanding the importance of context, setting and participants' frames of reference. They were also faced with ethical and methodological tensions and decisions about the impact of the Internet on what their participants said, how it was said and on the method and practice of online interviewing. Such research involved an 'epistemology of doing' (Teli et al., 2007) that emphasised the doing of technology, sustained interaction, and being online in order that the researchers could understand the everyday practices associated with the context. 'Typing and posting oneself into existence, researchers can earn the code, build communities, and collaborate with others.' (Teli et al., 2007) Researchers then can also become included in the epistemological space of the practice under investigation.

Advocates for social constructionism and philosophical hermeneutics might agree that individuals are 'self interpreting human beings and that language constitutes this being' (Schwandt, 2000: 198). However, hermeneutics take this a step further by trusting in the potential of language (conversation) and interpretive practice to disclose meaning that emerges within the dialogic encounter. This allows for the exploration of being (Illingworth, 2006) using qualitative research methods that draw on the interplay of making sense of, and interpreting, participants' voices and stories to construct knowledge of the dynamics of that situation. The unique strengths of qualitative methods of data collection are their ability to search for a deeper understanding of participants' lived experiences (Illingworth, 2006). Table 1.3 examines this issue in more detail by comparing the processes of knowledge construction in online as opposed to face-to-face interviews.

As Table 1.3 illustrates, the characteristics of both online and face-to-face interviews suggest that online interviewing will not be appropriate for all qualitative research. The methods should be considered based on the topic being investigated, how knowledge is to be generated and which methods are really best equipped to get at answers researchers are looking for (Baym, 2005: 231).

## Conclusion

This chapter has examined the theoretical concerns about how knowledge is constructed in qualitative research and the implications for online interviewing. It has discussed how knowledge is constructed in this disembodied, anonymous

Table 1.3 The processes of knowledge construction in online and face-to-face interviews

| | Online interviews | Face-to-face interviews |
|---|---|---|
| Cost | Cheaper to conduct. There is no need for transcription as there is a continuous and visible record of the interview.<br><br>However online interviews from home require considerable commitment from participants if they have to remain online for extended periods of time. | Greater costs incurred, for example, travelling to location for interviews and transcription costs. |
| Access | Allows access to individual/groups not possible to reach/interview by telephone or face-to-face interview or have geographically distant location.<br><br>However, only people with access to the Internet and/or have experience of online facilities/keyboard skills will be able to participate, particularly in synchronous focus groups. | Easier to exclude certain individuals/groups because they are geographically dispersed, marginalised or disabled.<br><br>It may be more difficult for participants with language/communication barriers to become involved in the research. |
| Temporal dimension | Asynchronous interviews are non-real-time and seen as an important part of online interaction.<br><br>Synchronous interviews are real-time. | Real-time. The immediacy of social presence that takes places when researchers and participants meet is a critical part of the research relationship.<br><br>The notion of social space includes temporal, physical, intellectual and interpersonal relationships. Focus groups can compound the effects of such factors, for example by individuals displaying particular attitudes, positions or status differences in front of other group participants. |
| Nature and speed of response | In asynchronous interviews, participants can reread what they have previously written, reflect on and consider their responses, enriching the text. However, there is also a greater risk of non-response. In synchronous interviews responses are spontaneous. | Researchers and participants can spontaneously share place and time to produce sensitive and in-depth data that reflects the interests of both. Non-response is also easier to observe. |

Table 1.3 (Continued)

| | Online interviews | Face-to-face interviews |
|---|---|---|
| Time | Provides the possibility to interview more than one participant/group at a time.<br><br>Asynchronous interviews can take several days/weeks. Synchronous interviews will be constrained by time.<br><br>However, external distractions can interrupt the flow of the online interview, of which the researcher may be unaware, resulting in the participant's temporary or prolonged disengagement with the interview. | Constrained by time pressures. But participants show less tendency to terminate the interview as and when they wish. |
| Venue and participation | Email/discussion board. | Venue plays an important part in influencing the interview process, taking place in settings that may involve the participant's home, the researcher's institution or more neutral sites in which the researcher has a physical presence.<br><br>Situating discourse within the physical location that is familiar to participants may enhance their willingness to disclose and hence the richness of data gathered. |
| Quality of data | The long period of asynchronous interviews can aid collection of in-depth data as it involves repeated interactions and closer reflection of interview issues. However, in asynchronous interviews that can continue for weeks, the researcher has to work hard to maintain rapport and probing | Visual and verbal cues are important social signals in face-to-face interviews and can establish rapport with the participant(s) especially if the participants are unknown to the researcher. |

(Continued)

Table 1.3 (Continued)

| | Online interviews | Face-to-face interviews |
|---|---|---|
| | as it easier for participants to ignore requests for further information especially if they do not wish to open up. In synchronous interviews the interaction and sharing of experiences is framed by researcher's and participant(s)' online presence. | |
| | Interviews do not have to be recorded thus eliminating participants' apprehension about speaking and being recorded. Transcripts are more likely to be accurate as participants can read what they have previously written in their responses and text cannot be misheard. However, conversational elements of simple gestures (nodding, agreeing, eye contact) have to be translated into text. | Interviews do not have to be recorded but this can affect the quality of the data in terms of breadth and depth. However there are greater opportunities for probing as it less difficult for participants to ignore/forget about requests for more information. |
| Identity and confidentiality | Reduces if not eliminates researcher/participant effects that result from visual/verbal cues or status difference (age, gender, voice, dress, disabilities, gestures). | Visual/verbal and status differences are present and may discourage/eliminate participants from taking part because of speech and mobility disabilities, or because they are shy/self-conscious. |
| | Participants can use pseudonyms so that their identity can be concealed from others. This may make it easier to discuss more sensitive topics or state unpopular views. | Participants may be less willing to discuss sensitive/personal topics because of the physical presence of the researcher. |
| | Guaranteeing participant confidentiality is more difficult to achieve especially in synchronous interviews, where postings and group discussions cannot prevent identification of the author of the message by others in the group. | |

and textual environment, and how that environment affects research relationships when the visual and verbal clues present in face-to-face conversations are absent.

It is evident that the Internet has the potential to open up a deeper view of life that is derived from real events and feelings as conversations, as well as exposing those experiences, which might otherwise not be heard or read. Researchers can draw on the observations of the rich and complex online lives of their participants to understand cultural meaning and highlight the complexity of daily social experience through online discourse and analyse situated behaviour (Wyn and Katz, 1997; Mann and Stewart, 2000). This has implications for 'how' and 'where' knowledge is constructed by individuals and, as researchers, how we make sense of social reality (Illingworth, 2006). Such debates will be examined throughout this book.

In the conduct of online research, the researcher is presented with many methodological and theoretical tensions because of its complex, diffuse and multi-faceted structure (Jones, 1999). As the book discusses, such tensions have implications for developing qualitative research projects using online interviews, not only in terms of issues around design, but in terms of shifting boundaries, the displacement of time and space, the nature of online interactions with participants, and the impacts of these practices and interactions on those being researched.

Qualitative research is highly personal and more contextual than quantitative research, and so the integrity of the researcher is crucial. Further, it is a holistic process in which participants share experiences and perspectives with researchers. When face-to-face contact is absent it is important to consider how this affects participants' knowledge construction and how researchers can be sure about the authenticity and identity of online contributions beyond what they are told by their participants (Hammersley, 2006: 8). This also suggests a situation in which participants are unsure about what to expect in online research settings. As we will see throughout this book, such issues raise methodological challenges, and exciting opportunities for researchers using online interviews, not only in the construction of knowledge, but also how that knowledge can be collected ethically.

## Practical Tips for Online Researchers

- Think about the implications of epistemology for your research practice.
- Decide what kind of knowledge you want to gather about the online world you are researching.
- Consider how you will justify your philosophical stance in online research.
- Think about how you are going to enter the online setting, the context of interaction and how you will communicate participants' experiences.

## Further Reading

Campbell, D.T. (1998) *Methodology and Epistemology for Social Science, Selected Papers*. Chicago: University of Chicago Press.

Crotty, M. (1998) *The Foundations of Social Research: Meanings and Perspectives in the Research Process*. London: Sage Publications.

Gilbert, N. (2008) *Researching Social Life*. London: Sage Publications.

# TWO

## Engaging with Research
## Participants Online

Overview: this chapter examines the nature of online relationships and communication in both naturalistic and constructed research settings. It will also examine different approaches to online communication and the nature of interactions that emerge between researcher and participant. Discussion will take place regarding the implications this has for collecting online interview data, as researchers attempt to not only make sense of their participants' social worlds in the construction of knowledge but also seek to sustain meaningful research relationships online.

## Introduction

Global expansion of the Internet has led to the growth of virtual communities in which the construction of knowledge emerges through relationships, roles, norms, institutions and language (Paccagnella, 1997). Understanding these social aspects of Internet behaviour is crucial for qualitative methodologies (Joinson, 2005).

This chapter examines how researchers interact with participants in the conduct of their online qualitative research. This concurs with our epistemological starting point that despite the absence of face-to-face interaction and a physical place in which to ground fieldwork, the development of research relationships and interactions online are still embedded in everyday lives (Carter, 2005). It is important to consider the nature of social interaction and communication that exists when gathering data on a one-to-one basis or in groups in the online setting, and how this affects the nature of participation in a research project (Preece, 2004). As researchers attempt to make sense of their participants' social worlds in the construction of knowledge, the chapter explores whether it is possible, using the Internet as a mode of research, to develop and sustain meaningful research relations, communication and interaction online.

## The Nature of Online Relationships and Communication

Early theories of Internet behaviour and computer-mediated communication have focused on the way in which the Internet affects interpersonal communication (Joinson, 2005). For example, Sproull and Kiesler (1986, 1991) gave a group of participants a series of tasks to perform via computer-conferencing systems and face-to-face. They found that the text-based medium of email removed social cues such as gender, race, ethnicity and age, as well as facial expressions and intonation routinely used in understanding face-to-face interactions. In the absence of visual and aural reminders, participants sent aggressive messages. The Internet affected interpersonal communication to the point of reducing self awareness and the awareness of others as a consequence of anonymity in online interaction.

Such models of Internet behaviour have since been criticised for not considering the different contexts in which online communities exist and how these contexts can shape the use of Internet effects (Hine, 2000). Tanis and Postmes (2005) argue that despite the inevitable decrease of non-verbal or bodily communication in comparison with face-to-face interactions, researchers need to consider the influence of social identity and deindividuation effects (known as the SIDE model). The SIDE model suggests that anonymity can induce a shift in focus from individual identity to social identity and have a positive effect on the social and contextual dimensions of community life (Spears and Lea, 1994). The decreased visibility of individuality can also shift the emphasis towards shared communalities and group concerns (Postmes et al., 1998).

The Internet then cannot simply be understood as technology with particular social effects. It must also be seen as a cultural context filled with rich and complex social experience (Hine, 2000). Rheingold's (1994) account of his participation with the Whole Earth 'Lectric Link (WELL) and his use of the term 'virtual community' has been critical in the recognition of the Internet as a cultural context (Hine, 2005). In participating in a supportive online group of individuals, Rheingold argued that online technology had the potential to establish a virtual community in which people came together and connected with each other, and it enhanced democratic participation. Bruckman (1992) and Curtis (1992) too in their work on the development of MUDs observed the social structures that emerged in these contexts. Consequently, what we have seen over the last decade is the emergence of online environments that have formed virtual communities that are multi-sited and bring forth different social constructs. This will be discussed more fully in Chapter 8.

The existence of online environments is brought about by people who share similar goals and values, suggesting that the nature of Internet communication can create different types of online interaction and social structures that are specific to different social groups (Joinson, 2005; Bishop, 2006). This highlights the meaningful social relations that exist in cyberspace and how communities are formed and sustained online. For researchers using qualitative methods of data collection, the establishment of online communities has opened up the possibilities of engaging in 'natural' as opposed to contrived research settings, in which participants can be observed in the field or site where social action takes place whether the researcher is present or not (Lincoln and Guba, 1985; Mann and Stewart, 2000). This has shifted the focus away from:

- Experimental studies on computer-mediated communication (Spears and Lea, 1994).
- Settings that are artificial and predetermined, rather than focused on the nature of the group or individuals engaged in the interaction (Baym, 1995).
- Research that is constrained by time (Paccagnella, 1997).

This means that online researchers can read messages and lurk the natural conversations and linguistic behaviour of their participants engaged in real-time chat without being noticed, intervening in anyway and revealing individual presence or intentions. Such covert participatory ethnography has been used to better understand the ways in which individuals engage in online environments such as MUDs, and the way they come to know people and create communities in an online environment (Isabella, 2007). Isabella found that by lurking in a MUD, she was able to experience it in depth, as a personal and social practice. This approach highlighted the ethical tensions of revealing her identity in order to collect her interviews. However, she discovered that the 'mudders' accepted her invitation to take part in the interviews because they knew her as a player rather than a researcher, and this played an important role in the construction of trust. This was also aided by the fact that she remained an elder of the game and her participants felt that she could truly understand their experience.

This approach raises a number of major ethical concerns that will be addressed in more detail in Chapter 5. The status of a lurker creates tensions for researchers who need to learn something about the online community but do not feel comfortable about fully participating. Online researchers are not the only lurkers. As Bishop (2006) argues, members of online communities may also observe the ongoing actions of other community members because they feel they do not need to post or because they do not have the confidence to fully participate and share their values. These lurkers, invisible to other participants as well as the researcher, can also represent a threat to the credibility of the research (Rutter and Smith, 2005).

This raises questions about how researchers capture the multi-faceted nature of Internet use and the kind of work that 'users do behind the screen' (Orgad, 2005: 58).

Online qualitative research relies on capturing the observable features of human interaction (Hine, 2000). This requires researchers to participate in order to check interpretations and gain participants' perspectives on the online interactions. Gatson and Zweerink (2004: 190) found that they were able to learn the communication style and norms of acceptability of the community without compromising their stance as observers. They argued: '…the Internet allowed us to move back and forth from participant to observer with an ease that being in sight for all interaction does not afford.'

By fully participating, researchers can regularly reply to postings in an online community and encourage members to share their views and beliefs (Bishop, 2006). However, another strategy for online researchers is to observe and participate in a limited way by making themselves known to the participants. Rutter and Smith (2005: 85) define this as 'presence and absence,' in which they '… did not hide, but we did not go out of our way to make ourselves conspicuous either'.

However, in participating in online communities, researchers risk influencing the behaviour of their participants. This is particularly so in online public domains in which posted information will not be private in the traditional sense of a personal conversation, but accessible for all to read (Sanders, 2005: 71–2). Conversely, the features of Internet interaction may encourage individuals to reveal more about themselves online than in real-life situations. The 'public space' in online communities can also be used to engage in 'private talk' (Joinson, 2005), an issue we will return to in Chapter 5. The form and dimension of communication then that takes place comes from the nature of interaction, and can be both purposive and incidental (Beaulieu, 2004). It is also influenced by the nature of the online setting which can encourage different types of text-based communication, including both asynchronous and synchronous communication. This issue is discussed in more detail in Chapter 4 but it is important to begin to reflect on the implications of such communication for how researchers and participants engage in the online environment.

Asynchronous communication is the most widely used form of online text-based communication on message boards and focus groups that are conducted in non-real-time at a conference site. Such communications can also involve one-to-one relationships between the researcher and participant via email (see Box 2.1).

---

## Box 2.1  Key features of asynchronous communication

- The asynchronous nature of text-based communication creates a new concept of time that is neither linear nor punctual and provides hypertextual links to other texts.
- Users of text-based communication can manipulate messages stored on their own computers for retrieval, editing and sending to others.
- Netiquette is an important component of online communication especially in virtual communities. (Kanayama, 2003: 269)

---

The key features of synchronous forms of online communication, as discussed in Box 2.2, allow for text-based interactions and have emerged through MUDs and MOOs. They have remained very popular forms of text-based real-time communication. Users can also access chat rooms available through applications such as Internet Relay Chat (IRC).

---

### Box 2.2    Key features of synchronous communication

- Temporal co-presence intensifies online interactions, thereby creating an atmosphere where discussions can flourish.
- The immediacy of synchronous online communications and chat leads to the expression of more emotive and heated exchanges.
- Synchronous written communications are seen as more oral, their linguistic characteristics mirroring the 'spoken' word. (Stewart and Williams, 2005: 405)

---

## Online Interviewing: Hearing and Locating Texts

When research using qualitative interviews is carried out online, researchers are seeking, through the exchange of texts, to glean something meaningful about their participants' lived experiences, through narratives and descriptions that will 'speak to the depths of experience, the meaning of relationships and the understanding of identity' (Markham, 2004a: 334). This is because researchers are interested in both *what* people say and the *way* they say it (Bryman, 2004: 321). Text-based online interaction requires active reflection and management of the very basic elements of the conversation, such as turn-taking, nodding or comments such as 'mmm' to denote that the researcher is listening. This is particularly evident in Markham's (1998) research using synchronous interviewing. In this she found that she wanted to react to her participants' messages 'nonverbally'. Markham comments:

> When I was interviewing Beth, I would ask a question and wait for what seemed like a long time for her to respond. Sometimes I didn't see writing on the screen shortly ... I would wonder if she had received the message. Then I would wonder if she was still there. Then to make sure she was there I would send the message again or another message asking if she got the first one. At other times after Beth would send a message, I would ask the next question ... and Beth's response would be a continuation of her previous message. In effect, I interrupted almost every story she tried to tell ... I felt compelled to fill the blank void with more writing ... Beth was chatting away ... I just couldn't see/hear it yet. (2004a: 335–6)

In trying to locate participants' texts, 'blank voids' and silences become an important and natural feature of the online interaction, just as they would be in a face-to-face interview. However, they often remain unnoticed, as also noted by

James (2007: 971) in her research where one of her participant's commented, 'About my professional identity *hmmmm* not a phrase I find it very easy to relate to …' suggesting a pause, and possibly some level of reflection in what has been written. As James found, it can become easy for online researchers to take these elements of communication for granted, or to ignore it completely. Yet they can provide a vital means of prompting and clarifying what has been written as the interview progresses.

On the face of it, online research can hide many personal and social characteristics, and thus can produce an impoverished form of social interaction compared with the richness of face-to-face communication (Giese, 1998). However, such characteristics may not always be as powerful in shaping conversations as the social presence of a researcher with participants, particularly in asynchronous communication. Given that embodied cues do contribute important information that can be used in understanding 'what is meant by what is uttered' (Markham, 2004a: 331), researchers have to think carefully about their online research design.

### Asynchronous and Synchronous Online Communications: Reflexive and Spontaneous Texts

Online interviewing at the most basic level involves an exchange of texts (Markham, 2004a). Yet, there has been much debate surrounding the richness and reflexive nature of the online medium. This needs to be considered by researchers in the conduct of their online interviews. Asynchronous email communications can allow for an extended and deliberate sequence of events and for researchers and participants to digest messages before replying (Kanayama, 2003). Participants have time and space to elaborate their own thinking, unhindered by the visual presence of the researchers, thus allowing for a thoughtful and personal form of conversation (Kivits, 2005).

Email communications can offer the opportunity for researchers to engage with the more personal aspects of participants' thoughts and feelings as well as with the more publicly visible. In terms of presenting themselves (Goffman, 1959) participants may be willing to allow researchers to access not only the 'front stage' area of their lives but also the backstage areas that are normally hidden from view. The semi-anonymity of online communications helps people to self-disclose more than it hinders them from doing so (Joinson, 2001). In online focus groups too, participants can interject brief statements of agreement into their communication to substitute for the absence of non-verbal communication (Schneider et al., 2002). Such conversations can be supported by conventional approaches to gathering qualitative data by using open or semi-structured questions supplemented with probes to explore and gain a deeper understanding of the emergent themes and issues (James and Busher, 2007).

The informality of online communication can facilitate a closer connection with participants' feelings and values. As Bowker and Tuffin (2004) note, the ability of participants to reflect on their thoughts and reactions can be enhanced as an outcome of the intimacy facilitated by the informality of typing. This became evident in our email studies (Busher, 2001: James, 2003). We found that the asynchronous nature of email communication encouraged the participants to immerse themselves in the communication. By using email to interview participants on an individual basis, we carefully followed each participant's online reflections and autobiographical voices, prompting them from time to time to help the constructions of their narratives. This was achieved by encouraging participants to review previous events through consideration of texts from earlier parts of their conversations with the researchers in order take forward their thinking on their professional practice and identity. We returned participants' texts to them as part of the normal email exchange – by not erasing messages from the exchange – allowing participants and researchers the opportunity to interrogate participants' texts as our dialogues developed. When issues and opinions were raised in the email exchanges they did not give the 'the right answer'. Instead, we asked more questions to help our participants 'reflect on a deeper level and get to the heart of the matter' (Russell and Bullock, 1999: 138). James (2007: 970) found that this led to her participants answering at a time convenient to them, sometimes not for days or weeks. One of her participants commented that he had not emailed back straightaway, but waited until he was ready to deal with the questions.

> I didn't email you straight back, because I was thinking about my answer. So my responses were more carefully thought through and probably longer than if I'd tackled the whole thing in a face-to-face interview ... again other ideas would probably not have come out because of the time pressure. This is what's good about the email process because ... it allows time to consider the questions and frame an appropriate response.

Such iterations are fundamental to the communication having a dialogic or conversational characteristic (Bampton and Cowton, 2002). Participants can explore and revisit their discourses by moving back and forth through their narratives, thinking about their responses, and drafting and redrafting what they want to write (see also Henson et al., 2000) at a *time* and *space* convenient to them, as discussed in more detail in Chapter 4. We also found that sometimes, the slower replies showed more powerful reflection on the main focus of the studies. We came to see such slow responses as an exciting element of the email process that created a level of anticipation and reinforced the point that 'One of the beauties of e-mail is that you never quite know when you will get a response ...' (Russell and Bullock 1999: 134). In our studies, this led to both researchers and participants spending time reflecting upon questions and answers as the interviews progressed, while the researchers also asked more questions to help the participants revisit their findings. In this process of reflection, the researchers' voices were also legitimated.

Email interviewing can create narratives that are enriched by the very fact that they represent the participants' constructed lives, thinking and reflections of their experiences. In asynchronous communications, there is more time for 'private self-focus' in which participants have a heightened sense of self-awareness through the act of having to focus on their inner feelings and emotions (Joinson, 2001: 189). However, in this process, researchers need to be aware that increased reflexivity can also have an emotional effect upon participants and the meanings they offer, particularly if the process is an uncomfortable one. Indeed, in James's (2007: 971) study, one participant shared her anxiety about being an academic, reflecting there was, 'no space for thinking about identity and coping with its loss'. In one-to-one conversations via asynchronous online interviews, a more in depth and reflexive text can be created. However, when research participants think critically about who they are, and engage reflexively in text and performance, spontaneity, which can be the basis for rich data, can become lost as participants elaborate on earlier responses to convey their changing perceptions (Bampton and Cowton, 2002).

In online synchronous communication, the exchange of text between researchers and participants tends to involve a dynamic form of dialogue that leads to a high level of immediacy and engagement with the topic being discussed (O'Connor and Madge, 2003). Of course this can be an advantage if the aim of the research is to create relatively spontaneous responses from participants and a high level of participant involvement. Further, participants who are reticent or shy in face-to-face contexts may find that they have more confidence to 'speak' freely (Rheingold, 1994: 23–4). Participants, who prefer more time for reflection, may find themselves lagging behind as the pace of discussion moves on quickly. The distinction between responding and sending can also become blurred as the interactivity defies conversational turn-taking. Bowker and Tuffin (2004) found that in their online synchronous interviews the delayed process of sending out questions and receiving participants' responses at a later time actually created less opportunity to relate with participants by reciprocating disclosure of experiences, although they met with participants offline prior to the commencement of the interviews to overcome this problem. Responses from the participants were brief (see Box 2.3).

---

### Box 2.3    Example of an online synchronous interview

Natilene:  if u don't mind me asking – (I feel very nosey asking u all these questions, but I never know what interesting tales u have to tell and what would be useful for my research) – how did they help?

Daniel:  ok, they helped me with info
Daniel:  I'm still on their email list
Daniel:  they provide good info
Daniel:  it helped me to know I wasn't alone. (Bowker and Tuffin, 2004: 235)

---

The 'temporal-co-presence' (Stewart and Williams, 2004: 405) that exists in synchronous communication also makes it possible for online texts to flourish. Participants can be more direct and spontaneous in their opinions and there exists a greater freedom of expression. This is particularly evident in O'Connor and Madge's (2003) research which conducted synchronous group interviews using Hotline Connect software with cyberparents to examine their use of a commercial parenting website. They found that for many of their participants this feature enabled them to ask questions without feeling self-conscious, which they might not have done face-to-face (see Box 2.4).

---

### Box 2.4   Example of an online synchronous group interview

Amy:   I feel better asking BW than my health visitor as they're not going to see how bad I am at house keeping!!

Kerry:   I feel the same. Like the HV is judging even though she says she isn't

Kerry:   Althoug my HV has been a life line as I suffer from PND

Amy:   Also, there are some things tht are so little that you don't want to feel leike you're wasting anyone's time. Askign the HV or GP might get in the way of something more important, whereas sending an email the person can answer it when convenient

Amy:   My HV is very good, but her voice does sound patronising. I'msure she doesn't mean it, but it does get to me…

Kerry:   Being anon means that you don't get embarrassed asking about a little point or something personal. (O'Connor and Madge, 2001: 15)

---

While the features of synchronous communications are dynamic and multi-threaded they do not allow for a rich form of social interaction. Nevertheless, the words that individuals choose, the sentence structures and linguistic features, whether composed asynchronously or synchronously cannot only encourage more expansive discussion, but give online researchers an insight into the frames that participants use to view the world, and the complexities of human expression.

In synchronous and asynchronous communications researchers and partici-pants can be active participants in the text, and choose to immerse themselves in the discourse, both emotionally and reflexively. A carefully considered reflexive response is just as credible as a spontaneous one, and can provide a more sophisticated understanding of the discourse that participants construct. The interactional nature of such texts still draws on conventional discourses, mannered behaviours and pre-interpreted meanings in which social categories are embedded. These may not be visible to the naked eye in the online setting, but they can be visible in the discourse (Seymour, 2001). These social cate-gories may serve to enhance the participants' communicative power, as we will discuss in more detail in Chapter 7, and in turn enrich the nature of the com-munication, as well as their 'social presence' (Schneider et al., 2002: 33).

## Conclusion

As researchers and participants interact with each other online, the texts they create both reflect and shape their understanding of their world. However, this process does not occur in a vacuum but is dialogic: 'cultural forms exist only through the exchange of messages and the subsequent adoption and reproduction of textual artefacts' (Markham, 2004b: 147). Online communication, is '... as complex, as varied and as individual as the people who engage in its exchange' (Davis and Brewer, 1997: 165), but it does not inhibit the communicative experience. Rather it reinforces a distinguishing characteristic of the medium (Duncan-Howell, 2007).

Yet, the removal of bodies from an interview changes the nature of interaction from orality to textuality, which is not a minor shift (Markham, 2004a). This means that the research relationship has to be continuously reformulated by researchers in order to make sense of the 'territory' (social space) of the online communication and interaction and reassure participants (James and Busher, 2007)

If researchers wish to understand in depth the experiences and identities of individual participants in their voice, then asynchronous modes of online communication such as email interviewing can at the very least generate more considered narratives and rich discourse that is reflective, analytical and creative, providing a depth that might be absent in uttered data. In contrast, synchronous modes of communication can offer performative, dynamic, spontaneous and open exchanges, particularly with groups of participants, and provide data that is more oral than literature (Stewart and Williams, 2005).

Computer-mediated communication offers a cultural context in which researchers can focus on the construction of reality through discourse and practice (Hine, 2000). It also provides a site for rich and sustained interactions with the field site and multiple ways of interacting with participants. These include both real-time and non-real-time engagement and observation. The latter approach also provides opportunities for the researcher to examine participants' points of view and construct thick descriptions (Geertz, 1973). While avoiding this interaction can have consequences for the nature of conversations that take place in the virtual setting, the researcher's presence can influence the manner of communication that takes place (Mann and Stewart, 2000).

Naturalistic online settings can provide opportunity for researchers to understand cultural meaning and the social experience of online discourse. But online interpretive projects will also take place in constructed contexts which researchers deliberately set up for the purposes of their research studies (such as online focus groups, email interviews and asynchronous conferencing). In these contexts, researchers can be in more powerful positions epistemologically than their participants, not least because they shape the agenda of the discussions. They will initially structure both the content of the messages and mode of discourse that takes place between researcher and participant(s). But as is evident in Busher (2001) and James' (2003) studies, participants can eventually take ownership of the conversations, express their opinions or share experiences and communicate detailed information with clarity and conviction. This highlights the strength of online communication because it makes available the active work of discussion as it is pursued through interaction (Bowker and Tuffin, 2004). It provides the possibility to give meaning to individual's lives and 'capture these meanings in written, narrative and oral forms' (Denzin and Lincoln, 1994: 10). However, as will be discussed in more detail in the next chapter, the nature of such communication can also involve hybrid virtual–physical worlds where 'face-to-face activities and physical artefacts meld with their online counterparts' (Ruhleder, 2000: 5).

## Practical Tips for Online Researchers

- In research design, consider the nature of social interaction and communication that exists in the online setting, and how individuals participate in that setting.
- Debate whether 'lurking' is a permissible activity and, if needed for your research, how you will use it ethically.
- Select synchronous or asynchronous modes of communication depending on the purposes of the research project.
- Decide whether the aims of the research are to produce spontaneous or reflective responses.
- Reflect on whether you will participate in an online discussion, and the ethical implications for how researchers announce their research identities and presence.
- Review the research relationship to make sense of the social space of the online communication and interaction and reassure participants.

### Further Reading

Crystal, D. (2001) *Language and the Internet*. Cambridge: Cambridge University Press.

Orgad, S. (2005) 'The transformative potential of online communication: The case of breast cancer patients' Internet spaces', *Feminist Media Studies*, 5 (2): 141–61.

Rafaeli, S. and McCarthy, A.Y. (2007) 'Assessing interactivity in CMC research', in A. Joinson, K.Y.M. McKenna, T. Postmes and U. Reips (eds), *The Oxford Handbook of Internet Psychology*. Oxford: Oxford University Press. pp. 71–88.

# THREE

## Developing Online Research Strategies: a Methodological Discussion

> Overview: this chapter examines qualitative methodologies and methods that have used online communications as a platform for collecting interview data. It also examines the opportunities for developing and understanding online research practices. This will include discussion regarding the conduct of virtual ethnographies. The chapter also considers the significance of combining online/virtual and offline/real interactions with research participants, and the methodological implications this has for online research projects.

### Introduction

In qualitative research projects, researchers have to consider not only the theory of knowledge embedded in the theoretical perspective but also the methodology – the process lying behind the choice and use of particular methods, and how these link to the desired outcomes. Such considerations prompt us to examine how the Internet can (re)shape online research, and the extent to which researchers can explore the Internet not only as a domain for investigation but as a site in which research methods can be adapted (Bryman, 2004: 473). Researchers' knowledge and understanding of Internet technologies is constructed by '... the methods through which we choose to know them and the underlying epistemological commitments on which those methods rely' (Hine, 2005: 7). However, when conventional research methods are employed in a virtual site that is faceless and are unbounded by time and space, the use of such methods may have social consequences for participants. Additionally, researchers cannot be sure that their participants' understanding of the Internet will be the same as theirs, nor can they be assured that their choices of the medium will reflect the experiences of their participants (James and Busher, 2006).

This chapter will examine qualitative methodologies and methods that have used computer-mediated communications as a platform for collecting interview data, and the opportunities for developing and understanding online research practices. This will include discussion of the conduct of virtual ethnographies. The chapter also considers the significance of combining online/virtual and offline/real interactions with research participants, and the methodological implications this has for online research projects.

## Qualitative Research Methodologies: the Question of 'Site' and 'Sight'

In seeking to understand human experience or relationships within a system or culture, different qualitative research approaches can be used to collect rich descriptive data and emphasise the possibilities of discovering new and unanticipated findings (Silverman, 1999). The rich content of such approaches, and their fluidity and flexibility also makes them adaptable to study a variety of research settings. One such approach is ethnography. Ethnography involves:

(i) An extended exploratory observation in which the research becomes immersed into a bounded community that becomes the focus of the study.
(ii) The scope for experiencing events and exploring the meaning of these events according to community insiders.

This places emphasis on studying 'first hand' what people do or say in particular contexts (Hammersley, 2006: 4). To study the culture of a community or group becomes an organising concept that involves a range of data collection techniques such as interviews and observation to understand people's experiences of community/culture (Mariampolski, 1999). To makes sense of culture requires the researcher to hear, see and write what has been witnessed (Van Maanan, 1988: 3). The 'legacy of the field' in ethnography (Clifford, 1997: 88) emphasises both the methodological and symbolic importance of the field as a site (place) where research is conducted and where researchers engage in 'real fieldwork' (see Box 3.1).

---

### Box 3.1  The 'legacy of the field' in ethnography

- A long-term involvement of the researcher among people/communities using a variety of methods to contextualise their lives.
- The ability of the researcher to become fully immersed into the community under study.
- The presence and interaction of the researcher in the social situation.
- Understanding the significance of the language and the actions occurring in the studied community.

---

The physical presence and interaction of the researcher provides a 'bodily element' to the research context (Seymour, 2001). It privileges visual, face-to-face encounters and incorporates highly personal elements. These include social conventions such as dress, status, use of language as well as the social characteristics of age, race, gender and organisational status (James and Busher, 2006). These are important signifiers which bring the participants into 'sight'. The centrality of the body plays a critical part in developing and maintaining social encounters. It influences the ways in which researchers and participants construct their identities and those of the other (Giddens, 1991) and how they assert their agency to make sense of the 'territory' (social space) of the social interaction in the face-to-face encounter. The potential of this approach then, lies in its ability to reveal context and complexity (Wittel, 2000). In this way as Eichorn argues: 'the legacy of the field not only continues to determine what constitutes fieldwork, but also shape people's research practices' (2001: 568).

Yet the idea of 'context' – the culture or community as a coherent entity, unique and different from other cultures, has become increasing difficult to sustain (Wittel, 2000). Cultures have been displaced through media development, telecommunications, computer-mediated communications, globalisation and migration (Giddens, 1990). Consequently, as Eichorn states:

> In a world where people's experiences of community and culture increasingly exist across geographic and temporal boundaries, ethnographers committed to understanding people's every day experiences on an in-depth level may need to abandon their commitment to place and face-to-face encounters. (2001: 577)

As discussed in Chapter 2, the development of the technological age has seen the creation of online environments as cultural contexts in their own right (Hine, 2000). This has led to a 'methodological shift,' and the 'claiming of the online context as an ethnographic field site' (Hine, 2005: 8). The methodological shift can be summarised by the move away from experimental approaches to research that were impoverished by the lack of a visual component towards the emphasis of social interaction in online environments (see Box 3.2).

---

### Box 3.2   The development of the Internet as cultural context

Phase 1. Psychological approaches to establishing knowledge involved experimental methods using quantitative instruments such as surveys and questionnaires (see for example: Sproull and Kiesler, 1986; Syniodinos and Brennan, 1988; Thach, 1995). Hine (2005: 7) describes this as 'an impoverished medium stripped of social context cues and therefore prone on the one hand to promote social inequality, and on the other to permit disinhibition and the display of aggression which would be deemed inappropriate in other media'.

---

Phase 2. An emergence of naturalistic and interpretive approaches to online research, in which the Internet is viewed as a cultural context through which '... ethnographic approaches have increasingly claimed online contexts as field sites in their own right' (Hine, 2005: 7). Such contexts are filled with rich and complex social experience which can be captured through the use of qualitative research techniques that place emphasis on the understanding of the social world through examining the interpretation of that world by its participants (Bryman, 2004: 266).

This second phase is particularly evident in the work of Hine (2000), who adapted traditional features of ethnography to study cultures and practices as they emerge through text-based, computer-mediated communication. She searched out websites concerned with the 1997 trial of a British nanny in Boston, contacted web authors by email and examined newsgroup communications. This adaptive ethnography offered a distinctive understanding of the richness and complexity of the Internet that included:

(i) The virtual object of study as a unique culture constituted in these environments as well as a cultural artefact of wider situated social practices.
(ii) Objects of study defined by their connections which infiltrated other spaces and times, thus disrupting the notion of specified-boundaries.
(iii) A move away from privileging certain modes of interaction such as face-to-face over online creating a 'field of relations'. (See Hine [2000] for a more detailed discussion.)

This approach has opened up the possibilities for a new field of research that shifts the focus from place to interaction, and location to movement (Markham, 2004a). In this approach, research can be conducted virtually, as opposed to always striving for a face-to-face contact with the field. This provides methodological possibilities for researching cultural dimensions of phenomena and social interactions (Dominguez et al., 2007). Traditional methods of fieldwork can be applied to computer-mediated settings to understand people's experiences. It is not always necessary to witness their everyday activities; to be 'on site' and 'in sight'.

## Moving Qualitative Research Online

It is in the social sciences that researchers have greatly expanded their methodological horizons, exploring the potential of ethnographic research in spaces where physical entry may not be possible. A wide range of research methods, such as interviewing, participant observation and focus groups have been adapted to collect rich, descriptive and contextually situated data in the online setting (Mann and Stewart, 2000). These methods have allowed researchers to understand cultural forms in depth and have involved participation in the online context. One of the first studies was that of Markham's (1998) ethnography of life on the Internet. This involved synchronous interviews, followed by a period of lurking in chat rooms and MUDs. Markham's approach highlighted the importance of the researcher's knowledge and representation of the context and participants, as she argues:

> Online, as interviewers we co-construct the spaces we study. This is not a minor point. Our interactions with participants are not simple events in these online spaces, but are constitutive and organising elements of the space. (2004b: 144)

Hine asks: 'how can you live in an online setting?' (2000: 21). Markham (1998) was both participant in and observer of life online. Despite the open questions or level of control she gave her participants to discuss what they wanted to, the life she was participating in was in part a product of her prompting, or constructing the very phenomena she was researching (Bryman, 2004). Such issues raise a number of methodological concerns that researchers need to reflect on when adapting their research project to an online setting, as raised by Fox and Roberts (1999):

(i)   In virtual communities there will be much ambiguity over the credibility of the participants' representation of a setting, the interpretation of these representations in written description, and the underpinning reality upon which participants' representations are based. (Fox and Roberts, 1999)

(ii)  It can be difficult for the researcher to maintain a stable presence in a virtual community when participants cannot see that the researcher is there. Offline, researchers will have lived in or worked in the field site, observed, taken photographs, asked questions and interviewed people in order to explore and understand their participants' experiences from their perspective. The researcher therefore has to decide whether to become a non-participant, investigating existing cultural artefacts such as home pages, be known but an inactive member of online communities, or become an active participant wanting to understand how participants construct social relationships within a virtual community.

For the online researcher, these concerns also present further tensions about the nature of the Internet as a valuable 'site' for research and the available methodological frameworks. They also raise questions around the ethics of online research and the issue of 'sight', as is discussed in more detail in Chapter 5.

## Doing Cyberethnography? Online and Offline Environments

Methodologically, the application of ethnographic approaches to the online setting has also led to a focus on the interrelationship between online and offline worlds. It raises questions about whether researchers should interview participants both online and offline (Markham, 2004b: 147). Virtual ethnography includes looking at wider social and cultural contexts (Hine, 2005). This has led researchers to challenge the view that 'online practice' should be the predominant concern of virtual ethnography, by exploring how it overlaps with the 'offline' in the making of ethnography itself (Teli et al., 2007).

In the past, the term 'cyberspace' has been commonly used to denote 'a field of interaction, existing in an independent reality separate from offline environments, bodies and concerns ...' (Kendal, 1999: 60). Cyberspace has rich and complex connections with real life and face-to-face contexts and situations (Hine, 2000). Miller and Slater (2000) in their fieldwork on the state of e-commerce in Trinidad, used several methods of gathering data including textual analysis of web pages and interviews with government officials, business owners, Internet service providers (ISPs) and ordinary users. They also hung out in the Internet cafes, chatted with people as well as sought out more formal and informal interactions with their participants. While their methods used traditional features of ethnography to study cultures, their research highlights how the processes of social interaction and communication in virtual space and everyday life can be intertwined.

In developing online research practice, Teli et al. (2007) have called for a move towards 'cyberethnography that stresses the hybrid and unfinished character of cyberspace ...' In adopting this position, they critique the label 'virtual ethnography' by arguing that in the 21st century ethnography is changing in relation to spaces, positioning and objects of study in cyberspace.

Some online researchers have argued that to understand life online you need to understand the broader context because 'being online and being offline are intersecting and interweaving experiences' that are influenced and shaped by cultural and social elements (Rybas and Gajjala, 2007). Identity is fluid and potentially multiple on the Internet, but people similarly engage in these practices in other areas of their lives and did so prior to the existence of the Internet. In other words, there is a 'connected space' in which individuals exist online and offline simultaneously (Kendall, 1999: 6).

However, to capture this connectedness requires a methodology that can research the connected spaces – the real-contexts and actions of the research participants and their exploits in cyberspace. To illustrate this the following study reflects the hybrid character of cyberethnography in which research can include both online and offline situations (see Box 3.3).

---

## Box 3.3  The hybrid nature of cyberethnography

Bakardjieva and Smith's (2001: 69) study examined how non-professional users of the Internet adapted and interpreted the Internet into the relevant structures and activities of their everyday lives. They wanted to adopt a

*(Continued)*

---

research methodology which would 'capture developments on both sides of the screen'. Their approach included adopting a structured personal interview, a tour of the computer and Internet-related space in the homes of their participants and the practices that took place. They also conducted a short group interview with the participants' family members about their understanding of Internet use.

This methodological approach helped the researchers to better understand how the technology of the Internet empowered their participants to transcend certain limitations of their situations. It also helped them to understand the spaces that were meaningful for individual and collective action and creativity. This meant that the research explored the making of boundaries and connections between the virtual and the real (Hine, 2000: 64). Their methodology involved them 'living at the intersections of online and offline' and highlighted the significance and particularity of the context ...' (Rybas and Gajjala, 2007).

### Research Design: Combining Online/Offline Interactions in Online Interviews

The desire to add credibility to research findings has often resulted in researchers making efforts to hold up the textual representation of the participants next to their physical personae (Markham, 2004a, 2004b). Researchers then mediate between the virtual field and the real field by combining online and offline interactions and communication in their research design by interviewing participants both face-to-face and online.

Researchers adopting this approach view it as a credible way of discovering the authentic meaning of participants' experiences. However, there are risks to be taken in combining both online/offline interactions to create a more meaningful enactment of an online space. Embedding online and offline spaces can be empowering (Orgad, 2006: 881). At the same time the interactions between online environments and offline spaces can be complex and limited. Some participants in online spaces will never have met face-to-face. In instigating face-to-face interactions, researchers actual threaten 'their experiential understanding of the informants' online world' (Orgad, 2005: 53).

To examine this in more detail, the following vignettes outline the methodological opportunities and challenges that combining online and offline interactions present to researchers and their participants. They draw on studies by James (2003) and Orgad (2005) that involved the researchers moving from asynchronous email interviewing to face-to-face interactions (in-depth interviews and conversations).

## Vignette: combining online/offline relationships – exploring academic identity

James (2003) examined academics' understandings of their identities and engagement with communities of practice both online and offline and how email interviewing could be recognised as a legitimate methodology. James was also interested in the way in which the compression of space and time online meant that geographically dispersed academics were no longer isolated from the context and traditions in which they worked.

This placed email interviewing within a 'virtual' ethnographic approach in which she attempted to '… gain a better understanding of the meaning that community members generate through conversation' (LeBesco, 2004: 63). This required her in a sustained interaction and 'being' online in order that she understood the everyday practices associated with the context being researched.

James's approach also placed the interviews within a more naturalistic inquiry in which she discussed the topics and the emergent themes with the participants offline. This was further influenced by the pre-existing offline relationships between the researcher and participants that were already interactive and influential through face-to-face contact with them in various arena of professional interaction. These offline relationships and social interactions informed her research design as she had already begun the processes of building trust and respect with her participants through them.

Away from the online space, she continued to discuss the research with her participants in face-to-face informal conversations (not interviews) to 'insert the online world of the Internet into offline contexts, and vice versa' (Hine, 2000: 115). For example, one of the researcher's participants mentioned in her email interview that she was concerned about losing her academic identity. When she met up with the participant at a meeting they were both attending, the participant talked about her experiences again. Later, when the email interview resumed, she probed some more by linking to things that had been raised in their face-to-face conversations. The move between online and offline interaction then, encouraged the participants to elaborate on their experiences, adding further threads to the email interviews. In this process, the researcher encouraged the participants to continue the processes of reflection that they were engaged in, online.

## Vignette: combining online/offline relationships – women with breast cancer

Orgad's (2005) study sought to examine and make sense of the meanings of Internet use in the lives of women with breast cancer as well as their everyday life aspects of coping with breast cancer. She used an exploratory site for identifying

*(Continued)*

(Continued)

the cultural dimensions that were important in the participants' lives. The researcher therefore sought to examine the connections between their online and offline experiences. However, Orgad (2005) did not know her participants, so in establishing relationships online she had to build trust to encourage them to collaborate and share their experiences with her.

After lurking for several months in breast cancer-related online spaces (which were predominantly North American), she posted messages on the breast cancer message boards inviting women to share their experiences of using the Internet in the context of their illness. To probe further, she then directly emailed women who provided their email addresses. Orgad (2006: 886) found that her participants, in contacting other patients who were geographically remote, constructed their online experience as 'cross-cultural and global' in which they shared 'emotional repertoire and vocabulary of meanings' (Orgad, 2006: 893).

Orgad (2005) also shifted her relationship offline using face-to-face in-depth interviewing. Of those who took part in the face-to-face interviews, she found that most participants were willing to open up and disclose their experiences. Orgad used the online exchanges to probe further in the face-to-face interviews, to follow-up on issues that remained undeveloped in the email interviews or address issues that had been omitted. She found that the participants' willingness to collaborate in being interviewed online and offline was largely due to the North American cultural context and the nature of communicative patterns and interactions that took place.

What these studies illustrate is the need for researchers to be clear about the methodological rationale for conducting both online/offline interviews, and to be sensitive in the 'transition from disembodied, anonymous and written interaction to an embodied and oral interaction' (Orgad, 2005: 61).

Such rationale can grounded in a set of criteria, which includes:

(i) context sensitivity;
(ii) flexible adaptation;
(iii) internal consistency and reflexivity. (Markham, 2004b: 146)

While in certain contexts it may be appropriate to supplement or verify data collected online with face-to-face interviews, this does raises questions about the *methodological precedent* of online research. Eichorn (2001) was faced with this dilemma in her study of women and 'zines (do-it-yourself magazines). Through constant reflection and sensitivity to the context, she adapted her methodology to achieve a stronger degree of internal consistency among her research questions and procedures. Eichorn realised that interviewing her participants in person was not appropriate because it was 'the absence of a proper locus that seemed to provide my research participants with a space in which to explore the aspects of their experiences and identities that otherwise remained interable' (Eichorn, 2001: 572). Illingworth (2001) also found that her participants were reluctant to participate face-to-face in research conducted in a clinical setting. Conducting the research online meant that the 'invisibility of women's experiences in this field were lifted, if briefly, as they became a central concern of the research process' (Illingworth, 2001).

These examples highlight the ability of online interviews to expand spatial boundaries. They offer participants the potential to communicate in a comfortable and physically safe environment (Mann and Stewart, 2000: 25), resulting in them feeling more in control of the interview process. The online space can represent a place 'beyond the context of their locale that transcends the social and cultural barriers that they encounter in their daily contexts' (Orgad, 2006: 893).

Whether research is conducted in sight or on site, the methodology has to be consistent with the integrity of the research topic and context, and researchers have to think carefully about how to convey 'the same level of confidence, commitment, privacy and trustworthiness in a "body-less medium"' (Seymour, 2001: 161). Markham (2004b) argues that centring the participant's experience in 'embodiment' ignores the researcher's embodied being. Ethically and epistemologically, it is important for researchers to reflect carefully on the extent to which the research design privileges them at the expense of the research context and sensitivity to the needs of the research participants.

One solution is to adopt an interpretive methodology, in which researchers 'see and sense' online interactions, as both analyst and experience-participant. This may help to remove the aura of suspicion surrounding stranger-to-stranger communication in cyberspace (Smith, 1997: 40). Researchers can have an active involvement rather than being a detached observer. This can lead to a sense of online belonging and, through that, a shared identity with their participants. This approach can also allow online researchers to delve into the everyday experiences of research participants, and attend to their voices, actions and emotions (Denzin, 1989), and can be usefully employed in the online setting, particularly when researching sensitive discussion through online group and one-to-one interviews.

However, it also indicates how hard researchers have to work to understand how their participants live and interact. Walstrom's (2004: 92) study of an online eating disorder support group found that her participants benefited from this approach in three ways:

(i) The representation of participants' own voices, validating their perspectives.
(ii) Thick description of their experiences shared by participants and enhancing their self-understandings.
(iii) A critique of the dominant discourses that structured and constrained the participants' ability to cope with the experiences, empowering them to realise potential change.

## Conclusion

Methodological approaches to online qualitative research have been broadened and reformulated across the social sciences to understand the complexities of the object of research and the different ways in which the object has been constructed (Dominguez et al., 2007). In particular, online interviews can offer unprecedented opportunities for qualitative research. They should not be perceived as an 'easy option' and researchers should give due attention to the justification, applicability and benefits of such methods to a particular research study. Researchers still need to think carefully about the methodological approaches they take, and the contextual, epistemological and analytical implications for the conduct of their online research projects (Orgad, 2005). They need to reassess the practices, expectations and requirements associated with fieldwork (Eichorn, 2001) if they are to mediate between the virtual and the real world.

Qualitative research can be achieved through online communication if 'the research is attentive to the specific sensitivities created by the virtual arena' (Sanders, 2005: 77). Meanings can still be created even when there is a physical distance between researcher and participants. This requires researchers to take personal responsibility to be accountable for the way in which they enter into the discourse and enable the formation of relationships. If online researchers' practice is reflexive and rigorous, the online environment can offer much in providing rich and insightful data.

The dilemmas of using online interviews as a research method in their own right suggests that further debate is needed regarding its methodological precedent. There is a need to examine in more depth the conditions under which online interviewing can be most effective, as well as the factors and techniques that enhance the credibility and quality of data, rather than simply including 'real' contexts as a way of contextualising findings (Hine, 2000). Over the next few chapters, we will begin to address these issues in more detail.

## Practical Tips for Online Researchers

- The practice of 'doing research' on the Internet points to a potential change in the way in which everyday life activities are performed. Reflect on the context of the research. Is it constructed, and if so by whom – the participants or the researcher?
- Ensure the research aims and design reflect the cultural context in which they are embedded.
- Think carefully about the effectiveness of transferring existing methodological frameworks online.
- Provide clear justification for your research strategy and reassure your participants about the methods to be used and how these link to the desired research outcomes.

## Further Reading

Fay, M. (2007) 'Mobile subjects, mobile methods, doing virtual ethnography in a feminist online network', *Forum: Qualitative Social Research*, 8 (3): art 14. Available at: http://www.qualitative-research.net/fqs-texte/3-07/07-3-14-e.htm. Accessed 10 December 2007.

Meho, L.I. (2006) 'Email interviewing in qualitative research: a methodological discussion', *Journal of the American Society for Information Science and Technology*, 57 (10): 1284–95.

Schaap, F. (2002) *The Words that Took us There: Ethnography in a Virtual Reality.* Amsterdam: Aksant Academic Publishers.

# FOUR

## The Displacement of Time and Space in Online Research

Overview: this chapter looks at the impact of the displacement of time and space in online research, especially through interviewing, and the implications this has for research participants. It considers how knowledge is constructed in a disembodied, anonymous and textual environment. The chapter also discusses how such an environment affects research relationships when visual and verbal cues are absent. It examines approaches to interviewing when conducted asynchronously and in real-time.

### Introduction

Time and space frames change, whether online or face-to-face. People use time chronologically to arrange space, such as interpersonal exchanges into a sequence and set them into a historical relationship with each other and other events (Gotved, 2006). But people also use the construct of time to regulate and give a direction to future actions and relationships, for example defining when people might meet or for how long.

In a similar way people use space to shape their own and others' understanding and construction of social practice. Spatial practice – what people do where and how that is described – is often linked to chronological time (Lefebvre, 1974, in Gotved, 2006). It is culturally constructed through time by members of a community (Lee, 2006). What is considered socially acceptable practice varies from one community to another. So, for example, how long it is considered polite to wait before replying to an email in an online conversation is not universally agreed. However, people's views of practice can be influenced by their membership of other communities, whether workplace-based or related to their social and family interests (Day, 2006).

Social designations of space also help to define what activities are permitted in particular places by people with the power to do so. The labels attached by societies or communities to spaces/places indicate how they may be (legitimately) used (Gotved, 2006: 478). How people talk about such spaces is a reflection of their cultural frameworks for making sense of space. The use of computers or websites may be constrained by social rules or conventions in particular places or at certain times. In online space some sites have open access, while others have restricted access. Terms such as 'chat rooms' indicate the social construction of how users think a particular space should be used.

This chapter considers the impact of the displacement of time and space in online research projects, especially in the construction of online interviews, whether carried out synchronously or asynchronously.

Although time and space can be collapsed in online exchanges, whether of a synchronous or asynchronous nature, some forms of space between communicators online may remain. For example, socialised space/distance (Allen, 2000) can exist even when people are physically proximate so it can also exist online. The nature of the physical environment (space) people encounter also shapes the activities in which they engage. For online processes this:

> can be the game world's geography, the threads of the newsgroup, or the frame around the chat ... it is defined primarily by the software (programs, protocols, services, etc.) and to a lesser degree by the hardware. (Gotved, 2006: 479)

The chapter therefore discusses how knowledge is constructed in a disembodied, anonymous and textual environment, and how that environment affects research relationships when the visual and verbal clues present in face-to-face conversations are absent.

## Interpreting Time and Space

Modern information technology makes it unnecessary for people to be co-present in a physical space to be either socially distant or proximate (Giddens, 1990). This is because people construct themselves by communicating or networking with others regardless of the physical space or time zone they occupy (Day, 2006). For example, the Internet is not simply '... a virtual space in which human actors can be observed. It is also a medium by which people produce themselves through exchange a wide variety of statements' (Bassett and O'Riordan, 2002) as people interact with each other. In asynchronous online conversations each (re)presentation of text can be separated by several hours, days or even weeks, but participants still feel they are present in a conversation. People construct multiple identities that alter subtly as they change contexts. These reflect the ways in which they position themselves in different social situations to fit within the boundaries of the particular community with which they are engaging at any one time (Zhao, 2006).

Spatial and time relationships between people are shaped by power, even if it is only the supposed norms of the particular group or community with whom somebody is currently talking. These relationships can be understood as power-geometries (Massey, 1994, in Rodgers, 2004) which are also shaped by the macro-cultural or societal influences on the community and on the people in that community. The boundaries of entities such as states and communities are socially and politically constructed by their members and influential others. Therefore they are provisional and open to reconstruction/reinterpretation. They are as much part of the internal world of these entities as of the external worlds that surround them (Derrida in Wolfreys, 1998).

People's identities, and their interpretation of the boundaries and power-geometries of time/space that surround them, change through time. They have to be negotiated by researchers if they are to engage with people in research projects. So researchers have to gauge what intrusions into their participants' inner spaces participants, individually and collectively, are likely to find acceptable or uncomfortable. This contributes to the construction of a small or micro-culture (Mittendorf et al., 2005) for a research project that reflects the relationships between its members. At its core is the development of trust between participants and researchers, which is discussed more fully in Chapter 8. It allows researchers to probe more sensitive areas of people's identities.

Micro-cultures are dynamic, reflecting the changing interrelationships between individuals, communities and societies where the nuances of power are played out (Rodgers, 2004). As all social relationships are 'bearers of power' the space/time relationships between researchers and participants have to be concerned with how time and space help to construct those power relationships (Massey, 1994, in Rodgers, 2004: 281), a view similar to that held by Foucault (1976). The social relationships that researchers construct with the participants in their research represent asymmetric power relationships. It is the researchers that initially set up projects and construct the rules of engagement with them for other participants. However, participants also wield power, even if it is only that to resist the demands of researchers.

Where participants are physically invisible to each other when conversing online, people risk misunderstanding each other. This is despite the texts they exchange containing evidence of their identification. However, these texts often contain crude labels that define participants' work or their person. These labels may have different shades of meanings in different cultures. So social distance and misunderstanding may arise between participants in a conversation whether face-to-face or online. This can arise because the words used by participants to write/speak about a topic may look familiar to their readers but carry different meanings in the different contexts in which the readers/writers are living. On such bases, participants are likely to assign different valencies (strengths) of power to each other, possibly incorrectly. This is because the valence they assign will depend on the cultures from which they come, not the culture in which the others are located. So participants' statements about their practices or their views of others' practices will be understood through the lens of the listener/reader's 'here and now' (Berger and Luckmann, 1966 in Zhao, 2006: 460). This in turn affects the authenticity of the interpretation of participants' statements that enable researchers to understand participants' actions in the context of spatial, temporal and socio-political and economic practices in which they are located.

In the constructed spaces of the Internet what interacts are researchers' and participants' constructed (re)presentations of themselves, their avatars. These may or may not reflect either their authors' views of themselves or others' views of the authors' identities in specific cultural or organisational contexts. A person's understanding and presentation of self is related to her/his 'here and now' (Berger and Luckmann, 1966 in Zhao, 2006). 'Here' is a person's construction of their current social and physical location, as well as their spatial practices. 'Now' is a person's current location in time as that person constructs it in her/his social settings. Such understandings are always in a process of becoming (Rodgers, 2004). They are not static but provisional, changing as the actors' relationships with others alter in the multiple contexts which they inhabit at different times sequentially and simultaneously.

How people perform online is framed by the social structures in which they are located. These limit and empower the actions people can take. In online interactions cyber social reality is shaped by online and socially located cultures, social and systemic structures (including the technologies of the Internet), and people's mediated interpersonal interactions (Gotved, 2006: 472). Performance is shaped by the 'here' and 'now' but also by its historical antecedents, its archaeology (Foucault, 1975). Performance includes speech and other representations of actions as well as physical actions. Speech includes texts, including the texts of online communication, as much as oral/aural interaction. Online communications are made up of a series of text–speech acts between a variety of participants, who could include researchers and other members of a research project. Understandings of performances, as well as their production, are shaped by the cultural constructions of time, space and social relationships held by the performer and the viewer or reader, the research project participant and the researcher.

Time both separates people, for example time zones, as well as bringing them together either physically or contemporaneously: I can co-habit a space with somebody at the same time and be physically proximate to them. Or I can be very distant from them but occupy the same period of time – and communicate with them online or telephonically. I can 'talk' with somebody from several time zones away and, if I do this synchronously, can write a textual exchange with them even if I cannot engage with them physically, face-to-face or orally/aurally. Online communications offer the opportunity for communicants to shift the time-boundedness of face-to-face conversations to time frames that suit themselves.

The allocation of time to activities is a social construction that is given different meanings in and by different cultures. Different times may be allocated different values in different cultures or by different religions: it may be difficult to engage in synchronous communications with some people, even if they are in the same time zone, during Friday prayers or Sunday religious services. Research participants starting their working day may feel it is inappropriate to engage in long reflexive research conversations when they have many tasks to address. Yet, the people with whom they are communicating synchronously are at the end of their working day and may be willing to engage in such discussions – unless they are pressed for time to get home for some reason. Communications may have to be truncated because of the values placed on the use of particular slots of time in participants' days. So negotiating the times of online exchanges across cultures needs careful consideration by researchers.

## Synchronous and Asynchronous Online Interviewing

The development of late modernity includes a development of the technology of communications that brings people who are locationally distant into synchronous interaction (Giddens, 1990). Online communications offer two modes for people to use: a synchronous mode and an asynchronous mode, as noted in Chapter 2. The former assumes that people are co-temporal, in contact with each other at the same time, even if they are not co-present in space. The latter assumes no coincidence of either time or space. In the former, participants may occupy different geographical locations and time zones (White, 2002: 257) but still be in contemporaneous conversation with each other.

### The Synchronous Mode

There is a heightened sense of immediacy in synchronous online communications, whether in social networks such as Facebook, or in online communities (Bishop, 2006; Williams, 2006), or in online research projects. Being in contact at the same time masks a plurality of lived realities. People in different international time zones may be in contact with each other simultaneously but be engaging in such activity at different times in their particular days (which includes evenings and nights). The lived reality of a person's 'here and now' is now supplemented by her/his immediate experience of the 'there and now'

(Giddens, 1990), of the distant but current, through the medium of online communication.

But they are not the same. Myopic assumptions confusing the 'here and now' with the 'there and now' are fostered by delusions of globalisation and of a 'global village'. Differences between people and cultural perspectives are glibly smoothed over in pursuit of a false notion of sameness. But this fails to acknowledge the underlying cultural and power differentials between people in different countries or areas of the world. Unless the participants in online conversations make explicit their different expectations of the use of time in their social spaces, such values and expectations are unlikely to become visible. Instead, implicit values and expectations are likely to shape the conversations, possibly creating misunderstandings and tension. Williams and Robson (2004) fear this might lead to complex interactions in which multiple conversations overlap and interweave. This in turn can present a chaotic narrative that can be confusing to interpret.

As online virtual environments, be they social networks or research groups, develop their interactions, participants develop a bounded and shared culture that describes how people should behave as members of that environment. This includes defining what actions people can take and when, how and in what manner they talk/text with each other, what topics can be talked about, and how the interactions of the group may be used outside the group (Sharf, 1999). So they develop their own order, their own goals and interests, and their own values, beliefs and language (Bishop, 2006). In turn this helps to define who can have membership of the community and who cannot and how that membership should be enacted.

### The Asynchronous Mode

Asynchronous communication allows people to respond to communications when they have time available. In asynchronous online research communications it is the 'temporal dimension' of the interaction that is important in developing relationships (Kivits, 2005: 43). It gives participants time/space to talk about themselves and engage with others at a speed convenient to themselves. Further this mode can address the problem of accessing dislocated and dispersed groups of participants, encouraging cross-cultural research (Murray and Sixsmith, 1998). The use of time and space also allows the online world to be inserted into offline contexts, and vice versa (Hine, 2000: 115), as explored more fully in Chapter 6.

In asynchronous communications, online sites provide a specific space where participants can send (post) their messages about a particular topic. These will be opened and responded to by other participants whenever they are online (Mann and Stewart, 2000). Such sites normally have either restricted or public (open) access. For example, asynchronous newsgroup communication means that participants involved stand, 'in a different temporal relationship to the messages, based upon their local exposure to them' (Rutter and Smith, 2005: 85). Where newsgroups offer open access asynchronous communication, their messages can be read by non-members (Stewart and Williams, 2005).

Asynchronous interviews offer researchers an opportunity to gain access to individuals or groups of people who are distant in various ways from researchers' primary places of work. We faced this issue in our research (Busher, 2001; James, 2003). Many of our participants lived in various parts of the UK while others lived in different time zones to each other and to us. It can also allow busy professional workers to engage with research who might not otherwise be able to do so (Bampton and Cowton, 2002). It removes physical distance between researchers and participants. It allows participants the opportunity to construct their narratives at a pace which suits them, unlike the constrained time and space they might experience in a face-to-face or telephonic interview. Yet the longer an online interview takes the greater the possibility that participants will become frustrated and drop out (Hodgson, 2004).

The creation of a social context in elastic time and space allows research participants to develop their views of a topic through time, revisiting their earlier views if necessary (James and Busher, 2006). This iterative process allows participants to move back and forth through their narratives, thinking about their responses, and drafting and redrafting what they want to write (Henson et al., 2000). So it allows participants to have time to consider their responses carefully and explicate how they '... live out their lives, find and maintain connections and seek to represent themselves to others' (Hardey, 2004: 12).

Through this process participants can take greater ownership of the construction of their narratives so they fit more closely with their own constructions of reality, while responding to the foci of a research project as indicated by the questions researchers ask. So participants experience a degree of positive affirmation (Bowker and Tuffin, 2004), while researchers hear richer narratives from their participants (James and Busher, 2006). Online group interviews offer a different dynamic, allowing participants to share and compare ideas with each other, and researchers to capture the outcomes of these social exchanges (Lee, 2006).

## Constructing Knowledge in Text-only Spaces

Knowledge in qualitative research is constructed through the social processes of researchers engaging with the other participants in their studies. This is part of the normal processes of identity formation in multiple social contexts that occur online and face-to-face in everyday life (Day, 2006). Constructing knowledge in online research takes many forms. Researchers can engage in one-to-one interviews or with participants in groups to investigate the social processes of existing online communities. Participant observation is acceptable so long as an online community agrees to it. Passive (non-participant) observation is usually not a means of research available to online researchers. However, researchers can engage in non-intrusive online research ethically (Walker, 2000). They can, for example, observe and analyse cultural artefacts on the Internet, such as website Home Pages, that are already in the public domain.

Knowledge construction is an iterative process. In research projects, it is facilitated through the data gathering and record keeping processes used. In online conversations, because of the nature of the medium of communication, language, rather than other signs and symbol systems, is at the centre of sense making. Participants' capacity to use the chosen language of communication without support from a variety of non-verbal gestures and visual clues constrains the quality and complexity of this sense making. The features of electronic text/chat, which might also be described as speech/writing, combine the 'permanence of writing [with] the synchronicity of speaking' (Zhao, 2006: 462). This occurs even when that exchange of speaking/writing is asynchronous. The archiving of such texts captures the flow of the conversation. They can also be made continuously visible to participants if a moderator does not delete email exchanges or website/message board postings. The continuous and visible record of online exchanges enables participants to revisit issues that slip temporarily out of view through the course of a conversation (Russell and Bullock, 1999). Participants and researchers can return to earlier aspects of an interview at their convenience and remind themselves of their earlier interpretations of their lives.

Given the limited research methods literature available to us on email interviewing at the time of our studies (Busher, 2001, James, 2003) we adapted conventional frameworks of qualitative research to meet the needs of the online medium (see Boxes 4.1 and 4.2). Participants were instructed not to erase any exchanges and to answer at the top of each message/question we sent to them. The request not to erase exchanges was to ensure that the researchers and the participants had a continuous record of the conversation to which they and we could refer. In a few cases where people did erase previous exchanges we had to use a cumbersome process of cutting and pasting their messages to our electronic records to keep the records of their exchanges with us in a chronological sequence. The request for participants to answer above the message/question sent to them was to allow the most recent aspect of our discussion to be at the most accessible point in the email messages that bounced backwards and forwards between us.

# Box 4.1 Rubric for engaging in online interviews about becoming a doctoral student

**Reasons for carrying out this study**

This arises out of a real problem that I have observed over a number of years: the difficulties which new students have in adapting to the demands of doctoral studies in English universities. These difficulties seem to be compounded when the students are already experienced practitioners in their field, are part-timers and have English as their second or third language. When the part-time students are based outside the UK and not in other institutions of higher education, then the problems of constructing a suitable work-related identity for pursuing doctoral studies in an English university seem very great.

This study seeks to explore how students construct their academic work-related identities and how their understandings of English for academic purposes, of the cultures of English universities and other universities, and of their own selves and future selves shape those.

Using email interviews for research is a relatively unknown field, so I am interested to explore it.

- As I cannot come easily to interview you and talk about the problem outlined above, I am trying to gather the data by email interview.
- If you are willing to be part of this study, please reply to this email straight away, confirming the appropriate confidential email address for this research.
- Discussion with you will be in the strictest confidence and participants' names will not be revealed in any documents or papers developed from this research, or to any other participants in this research.
- You will be asked nine substantive questions, as well as a few biographical ones at the beginning, and a question evaluating this email research process at the end.
- The substantive questions will be sent to you one at a time for you to comment on and respond to. Each question may be followed up by supplementary questions. This process simulates a face-to-face semi-structured interview.
- Please answer on top of the message and question sent to you (not at the bottom of it!). This is to sustain the sequence of question and answer in our discussion, without both of us having to scroll through screeds of earlier dialogue – although you are welcome to make reference to our earlier dialogue in you answers to current questions.
- Please do not delete any part of the email dialogue as it develops – it is your (and my!) record of our conversation.
- Please reply to each communication within three days.
- Our whole email discussion is expected to be completed within three weeks.
- Many thanks for your help and time with this (pilot) project. (Busher, 2001)

# Box 4.2 Rubric for conducting interviews with academics

A little while ago you completed a questionnaire, which focused upon professional identity, how it is managed within the professional environment and whether it is possible to generate a common sense of identity across the psychology profession. You agreed to take part in an email interview, which will address the issues raised in that questionnaire. Please read the following guidelines and if you are still happy to take part in the interview, please reply to this email and I shall send you the first question. The email interviews will consider the issues that arose in the questionnaire in more depth. The data gathered through the email interviews will provide a transcript of your account. These accounts will be used to inform the research study.

In undertaking the email interview please note the following guidelines:

(i) If you are still willing to take part in this study, please reply to this email straight away.

(ii) The interviews will be conducted in strictest confidence and your anonymity will be assured throughout the research project.

(iii) You will be asked 11 substantive questions.

(iv) These questions will be sent to you one at a time. Please respond to the question by email. Each question may be followed up by supplementary questions.

PLEASE DO NOT ANSWER AT THE BOTTOM OF IT. This will ensure the sequence of questions and answers is not broken.

(v) It is anticipated that an ongoing dialogue will occur. In order to achieve this, please ensure that you answer on top of the message and question sent to you.

(vi) Please do not delete any part of the email dialogue. This will be our record of the conversation.

(vii) Please reply to each email question within three working days if possible. I will also try to reply to your response within that timescale.

(viii) It is anticipated that the email dialogue will be completed within ten weeks.

(ix) Once the dialogue is complete you will be asked to authenticate your account.

(x) The completed dialogue may be followed up by further email discussion. (James, 2003)

Through these rubrics, knowledge construction developed through the relationships we formed with our participants. These went beyond stereotypic roles of question-asking and question-answering (Oakley, 1981) into a more collaborative approach to research. This allowed participants to influence the development of a project and so have a sense of ownership of it (Bakardjieva and Feenberg, 2000). Collaboration goes beyond notions of informed consent to participation and to dialogic engagement with a project. It helps researchers to gain rapport with their participants (Bakardjieva and Feenberg, 2000).

This approach is methodologically important 'because as interaction constructs and reflects the shape of the phenomena being studied, interaction also delineates the being doing the research in the field' (Markham, 2004b: 147). Consequently, as participants begin to take greater ownership of the text-only space of Internet communications, they gain the confidence to respond to researchers' questions in unexpected ways and directions. In our studies we responded to the new directions of their narratives rather than only keeping to the agenda of the original interview schedule. The latter would have enforced our control of the interview process and might have closed off the rich narratives that were emerging.

The Internet provides a new space for engaging in communication. Exchanges in this medium are largely devoid of the normal social frameworks of face-to-face encounters. So, unlike in face-to-face encounters, participants are deprived of the vocal, verbal or non-verbal cues of gesture, tone of voice and facial expressions to help them interpret the meanings of the other. However in face-to-face conversations, understandings can be distorted by the social characteristics of the other participants. People shape their responses to fit their interpretation of the characteristics of the other and make assumptions about what the other might want to hear (Sproull and Kiesler, 1986; Mann and Stewart, 2000).

If the presence of social signals is often problematic for participants and researchers in face-to-face qualitative research, so is their absence. Non-verbal and contextual elements are often seen as essential to facilitating interpersonal engagement in interviews. However, these are often absent in online conversations because of the use of text-based interactions. So online researchers using qualitative methods have to use different ways to build trust and encourage participants to 'open up' (Knight and Saunders, 1999). In our studies, some participants commented adversely on the lack of personal contact inherent in the email interview process.

However, the absence of social and contextual cues can also be beneficial in research. In online communication concealment of participants' social characteristics appears to aid self-disclosure and social interaction (Lee, 2006; Joinson, 2001). In online group discussions where social context cues are missing, '... people can't "see" the boundaries that divide them, so will tend to participate more equally ...' Kiesler (1994: 11). Online communication appears to provide a shield (Mann and Stewart, 2000) that facilitates disclosure between participants. It leads Lebesco to interrogate the nature of: 'communication from the body in spaces devoid of faces' (2004: 75). The apparent invisibility of participants' bodies in text–space and its impact on the identity work that takes place in it is examined in Chapter 6.

A factor in constructing participants' knowledge of the other in Internet research seems to be the speed or certainty with which messages are answered. In our studies, slow responses by researchers to participants' queries appeared to weaken some participants' sense of engagement with the research conversations. This seemed to undermine their expectations of what they thought it meant to be engaged in a research project, or of the way in which they expected researchers to act.

Conversely, in asynchronous conversations participants are able to answer at a time convenient to themselves. In our studies, some participants' responses took weeks or months, initially we found this very disquieting as we had not expected it, and wondered whether participants had dropped out. So new norms of discussion that legitimated these new understandings of the processes of online interviews had to be tacitly negotiated with participants. In our studies we eventually came to see the erratic speed of responses as an exciting element of the email process because we never quite knew when we were going to get a response from whom.

So the environment in which research interactions take place has considerable influence over the outcomes of those interactions. Researchers and participants construct this environment through their interactions, and negotiation of the processes, modes and tone of engagement. Initially, in a research project, it is the researchers who shape this environment whether online or face-to-face. However, participants can also take control over the direction of the interviews or discussion as has previously been illustrated. So knowledge and construction of process, as well as of substance, is shaped by the flows of power in social situations. Some people have greater power than others in a situation to enforce their definitions of it (Foucault, 1975). Naively, when we began our studies we thought 'email brings people into contact ... and places each on equal ground' (Boshier, 1990: 51) and considered that email had the potential to democratise narrative exchanges (Illingworth, 2001). Power in online communities and research projects is discussed in more detail in Chapter 7.

Another issue facing online researchers is whether the responses of participants are actually their own thoughts (Chen and Hinton, 1999). In our studies we assumed that because our participants responded to us on their usual email addresses, it was they who were responding. Nonetheless, the absence of visible cues makes it difficult to know who is talking in an online conversation. Further, although certain elements of emails and other online postings, such as headers and signatures, appear to indicate the origin of a message, the real origin and authorship of messages can be hidden with relative ease (Lee, 2006).

So knowledge of who is speaking in online communications has to be sought within the confines of text-space. This includes the recognition of regularities of speech patterns, means of expression and responses to particular events or the views of others; a process similar to that in face-to-face relationships (Whitty, 2002). People develop various styles of interaction through their use of language/text which help to distinguish them from other participants in online conversations. So the more people engage in online conversations in particular communities, the more other members of those communities come to recognise and build up trust in their knowledge of the other participants. However, this does not indicate that people's online persona accurately reflects their offline identities as we discuss in Chapter 6.

If such knowledge is difficult to ascertain in online research, so is the nature of participant validation of data records. Online researchers can never be entirely sure to what depth participants in their studies actually agree with the records of their exchanges with the researchers. In contrast, what really matters is participants' view of the truthfulness of their answers and whether they are satisfied that they are adequately represented by them (Hine, 2000). Time lapses in message exchanges in online interviews can make this problematic if participants cannot remember what they had said previously. For example, one participant in our studies pointed out that 'in email communication clarification is not always easy' (James, 2007: 969). However, the problem of authenticating participants' records in online research is mirrored by a similar problem in face-to-face communications (Carter, 2005). The doubtfulness of linkages between participants' voices and researchers' interpretations of the themes emerging from them can be reflected in the way in which studies are analysed (James and Busher, 2006).

## Conclusion

The flexibilities of time and space in online research make it possible for researchers to engage with participants whom they might not otherwise have reached. However, the technologies of the Internet also restrict the range of people with whom researchers can engage. This potentially disempowers a very considerable number of people in the world in all societies, but especially in economically poorer societies, from taking part in online research. Through the Internet researchers are likely to talk with a very select group of people that may be unrepresentative of the views of many others.

The capacity of the Internet to allow people to construct understandings of a 'there and now' (Zhao, 2006) as well as a 'here and now' must not be allowed to lure people into imagining that the 'there' is the same as the 'here' because of the different micro and societal cultures in which people are embedded in their work communities. These cultures are likely to shape the ways in which participants will be willing to respond to conversations with and questions by researchers. They will affect the language people choose to use as well as the topics on which they may be willing to talk. They will shape the ways researchers are perceived and the ways in which participants perceive each other. This will shape the stories that people are willing to tell and the degree of conversational intimacy in which they are willing to engage.

So the construction of knowledge in the disembodied text-space of online research is problematic. However the problems are not insurmountable. Many of the ways in which people establish the authenticity of other people's communications is through recognising the patterns of their speech and thinking. This can be largely replicated in engaging with people's online text/speech acts. The non-verbal and contextual signals of face-to-face conversations provide useful scaffolding to facilitate understanding between people. However, their absence is not an unmitigated disaster in online communication. As will be discussed in Chapter 8, people develop other ways of shaping text to achieve similar support.

## Practical Tips for Online Researchers

- Discover what time zones your participants inhabit and the extent to which their patterns of work mirror yours.
- Discover when it is most convenient for your participants to respond to your questions.
- Explore your participants' cultural understandings, hopes and fears of Internet communication.
- Allow your participants to shape the process and direction of conversation so they have a greater sense of ownership of the research.
- Be sensitive to the values, aims and interactions of people in different virtual environments.

### Further Reading

Gotved, S. (2006) 'Time and space in cyber social reality', *New Media and Society*, 8 (3): 467–86.

Janelle, D.G. and Hodge, D.C. (2000) *Information, Place and Cyberspace*. New York: Springer.

Madge, C. and O'Connor, H. (2005) 'Mothers in the making? Exploring liminality in cyberspace', *Transactions of the Institute of British Geographers*, 30 (1): 83–97.

# FIVE

## Dealing with Ethical Issues

Overview: this chapter examines a range of ethical debates that researchers must consider in the conduct of their online research projects. These include the complexities of delineating public and private online spaces, as well as consent and accessibility, trustworthiness of the data, confidentiality, privacy and security, and netiquette. It also focuses on inequalities, language and power relations. The chapter discusses how ethical principles associated with onsite (face-to-face) interviews can be translated for qualitative online research, especially when collecting sensitive and personal information. It also considers the influence of cross-cultural studies on the ethics of research.

### Introduction

The Internet has altered the nature of the context in which research can take place and how knowledge is constructed. It has created opportunities for researchers to carry out fieldwork in online contexts, allowing them to construct international research projects without leaving their offices. Conventional methods of on-site social science research have been adapted to the online environment, but this has meant that researchers are faced with new contexts in which to resolve the ethical problems of research.

Online research uses many different research methods to span many distinct socio-cultural boundaries. Each society will have its own approach to what might constitute ethical research and the distinctive nature of virtual reality. Consequently there is a need to develop understandings of what might constitute ethical Internet research in cross-cultural settings. These understandings need to reflect the 'ethical pluralism' of the world, as well as of the Internet, where there is a continuum of legitimate ethical choices available to online researchers (Ess, and the Association of Internet Researchers [AoIR], 2002: 181–4). These choices are guided by different ethical and philosophical frameworks (deontological, utilitarian, virtue) (Ess, 2004: 254).

This chapter examines a range of ethical dilemmas that emerge when using the Internet as a site for qualitative research interviews. There is still widespread debate about what constitutes appropriate online ethical conduct (Johns et al., 2004). These include ambiguities around public/private spaces,

netiquette and informed consent, protecting privacy and anonymity, confidentiality and data security, and the trustworthiness of data. These discussions
raise issues about how participants and readers of research can have some cer-
titude about the credibility of the outcomes of research. However, at present 'there is no simple rule for getting right the balance between potential
risks to participants and benefits of the research to a wider community'
(Economic Social Research Council [ESRC], 2005: 25). The chapter begins by
considering what constitutes an ethical framework of research and its implication for studies using qualitative methods.

## An Ethical Framework for Research Using Qualitative Methods

The ethics of research has two major purposes. One is to ensure that receivers of
research can be confident that the outcomes of research can be trusted. The other
is to ensure that society's benefit from research is not at the expense of individual participant's engagement with them. 'Research should be conducted so as to
ensure the professional integrity of its design, the generation and analysis of data,
and the publication of results' (ESRC, 2005: 23). Further, 'the direct and indirect
contributions of colleagues, collaborators and others should also be acknowl-
edged' (ESRC, 2005: 23). The 'moral consequences' of our actions as researchers
need to be considered in terms of research conduct and responsibility (Knoebel,
2005). All research should be conducted with an ethic of respect for:

- the person;
- knowledge;
- democratic values;
- the quality of educational research;
- academic freedom. (British Educational Research Association [BERA], 2004: 6)

This is because researchers face ethical dilemmas at every step in a research
project (see Box 5.1).

---

**Box 5.1   Where ethical dilemmas occur in the research process**

- The nature of the project itself.
- The context of the research.
- Procedures adopted.
- Methods of data collection.
- Nature of the participants.
- The type of data collected.
- What is done with the data and how it is disseminated. (Cohen et al., 2000: 49)

---

The principles or standards that guide the proper conduct of research are enshrined in codes of professional research conduct. These codes are intended to protect the rights of participants and to ensure that no harm comes to them in terms of their privacy, anonymity and confidentiality (see Box 5.2).

---

### Box 5.2    Aspects of harm from which to protect participants

(i) Personal social standing, privacy, personal values and beliefs, including the adverse effects (to them) of revealing information that relates to illegal, sexual or deviant behaviour.
(ii) Links to family and the wider community.
(iii) Position in occupational settings. (ESRC, 2005: 21)

---

A key element of these codes is the voluntary engagement of participants in research. Participants are expected to give their informed and explicit consent to take part in research. Their consent should be free from coercion or bribery. Researchers should inform them of 'their right to refuse to participate or to withdraw from an investigation' (ESRC, 2005: 7). Where research involves vulnerable groups of people, such as children, informed consent may need to be managed through a proxy. This person should either have a duty of care for the potential participants or provide 'disinterested independent approval' (ESRC, 2005: 7). Box 5.3 sets out one construction of the grounds for informed consent.

---

### Box 5.3    Grounds for informed consent

(i) Participants being in a position or old enough to understand the choice that they are making.
(ii) Researchers fully disclosing the purposes of research.
(iii) Researchers fully disclosing any risks to participants.
(iv) Participants understanding that and being able to withdraw at any time from a project. (Cohen et al, 2000: 51)

---

So before undertaking a project, researchers need to know why they want to research a specific topic, of what use the findings might be, and what might be the potential moral or ethical issues in carrying out the study (Sikes, 2006). Whatever research paradigm they choose, researchers will need to construct a rigorous methodological framework to meet the epistemological purposes of their proposed study. In this way they will construct trustworthy outcomes to their project that will benefit society.

At the start of a project researchers will need to convince participants of their integrity and competence as researchers. One means of doing this is to create an explicitly ethical framework in which to conduct their research. Another means is to develop positive personal relationships with participants. Visible social characteristics (age, race, gender and organisational status) of researchers and participants, expressed through verbal cues in online conversations, are likely to distort the outcomes of research conversations. Although possibly less influential in online research, peoples' names and aspects of biography that researchers might give to potential participants in beginning their research projects are likely to be interpreted by participants, as Mann and Stewart (2000) point out. This is likely to influence participants' responses to researchers and the progress of a research project, at least in its early phases.

Some types of research make people 'vulnerable' (ESRC, 2005), for example, any research likely to cause harm even if unintentionally, or research requiring deception or conducted without participants' full and informed consent at the time the study is started is said to make people vulnerable (ESRC, 2005: 8). In cases where deception is an essential part of the research design, researchers are expected to make participants aware of what procedures have taken place immediately after the research has finished (BERA, 2004; British Sociological Association [BSA], 2002). Further, they should be prepared to support any participants who are distressed by the loss of trust that may result from this. Similarly, research that induces psychological stress, anxiety or humiliation, or causes more than minimal pain or involves intrusive interventions (ESRC, 2005: 8) makes participants vulnerable. Such research is likely to deal with sensitive topics such as participants' illegal or political behaviour, their experience of violence, their abuse or exploitation, their mental health, their gender or their ethnic status. Any research that requires access to records of personal or confidential information, including genetic or other biological information, makes participants vulnerable.

Where groups of people are deemed vulnerable, it can be difficult for researchers to be sure that they have gained their voluntary and informed consent to take part in a research project. Such groups include members of custodial, or health and welfare institutions, children and young people, and those people with a learning disability or cognitive impairment, or individuals in a dependent relationship with the researcher. With these groups, the permission of a gatekeeper is normally required for researchers to gain access to them.

Qualitative research methods are potentially revelatory as the words participants use, the way they position themselves, or the position they hold in an institution can make them identifiable. The capturing of visual data compounds this visibility. Case studies and postmodern and post-structural studies normally site their participants explicitly in their socio-political, organisational and economic contexts. This risks destroying the privacy and anonymity of the participants, breaching the ethical guidelines set out above. It might also result in harm being caused to some participants if powerful people in their environments disagree with views they express to researchers. Researchers need to be sensitive to the socio-political contexts and communities in which individuals' live out their lives as ethical problems may emerge from participants' interactions with their contexts.

Ethical research must avoid contravening the rights of the researchers and participants involved while allowing society to gain benefits from it (Cohen et al., 2000). To construct such research, researchers must engage in a dialogue with the social moral frameworks of the society in which their study is carried out, whether codified or not. Such dialogues intersect with researchers' own moral predilections and views (Busher, 2005). Researchers can themselves be at risk from unethical practice by other participants, whether intentional or not. They should not risk causing harm to themselves by any actions they take with other participants or in the contexts in which the participants are located (ESRC, 2005: 25).

Constructing ethical research 'is not purely a function of the application of ethical codes of practice' (Usher, 2000: 162) but an imminent or emergent ethical practice for researchers throughout their projects and beyond, when writing up. They have to balance the needs of participants, society and themselves by using a variety of technologies: ethical frameworks, ontological and epistemological perspectives, and research methods and techniques. This raises issues about the adequacy of conventional offline ethical frameworks for conducting online research interviews (Hookway, 2008), and how such interviews might be designed and implemented to meet the needs of participants and other people interested in the process and outcomes of the research.

## Ethics in Online Research Interviews

The Internet offers online researchers means of addressing research agendas that might not be possible in face-to-face research. Yet they still have to ensure that research is carried out with professional integrity and an ethical respect for its participants. However, it may not be so easy to apply recognised codes of ethical conduct for onsite research to online time/space. As the Internet 'blurs the traditional boundaries between interpersonal and mass communications, ethical concepts like privacy and dignity of participants become more difficult to determine' (Delorme et al., 2001: 272). Online, researchers may be temporarily, physically and culturally distant from their research participants as well as co-temporal and co-spatial, if not co-present

(Giddens, 1990). They may conduct synchronous and asynchronous research interviews to collect data which they might store electronically as well as physically in a number of ways.

In the virtual space of the online interview, researchers face a range of ethical issues 'in their efforts to acquire new knowledge about many behaviours and practices that arise in these new venues' (Ess, 2004: 253). Online research entails greater ethical risk to individual privacy and confidentiality, greater challenges to a researcher in gaining informed consent, and more difficulty in assuring and ascertaining trustworthiness and data authenticity (Ess and the AoIR, 2002; National Committee for Research Ethics in the Social Sciences and the Humanities in Norway [NESH], 2003, 2006). Researchers have to address the issues of, 'privacy, confidentiality, informed consent, and appropriation of others' personal stories' (Sharf, 1999: 245). Indeed, especially in Internet-based research, 'the issues raised [are] *ethical* problems precisely because they evoke more than one ethically defensible response to a specific dilemma or problem. *Ambiguity, uncertainty, and disagreement are inevitable* [sic]' (Ess and the AoIR, 2002: 4, original emphasis).

To try to resolve these conflicts, Acceptable User Policies (AUP) are now being produced by bodies with a professional interest in the use of the Internet. This includes the AoIR, established in the USA, and the NESH. The Computer Ethics Institute in the USA offers 'ten commandments' (Robson and Robson, 2002: 98) about how users of the Internet should not cause harm to other people (see Box 5.4). Commandments 1, 4, 5, 8, 9 are directly relevant to researchers engaging with participants in online research. Access to people's email addresses, as well as access to participants' views on a variety of subjects places researchers in a very powerful position vis-a-vis participants. It is important that researchers consider carefully the responsibilities that this access to knowledge gives them.

---

### Box 5.4    The 'ten commandments' of computer ethics

- Thou shalt not use a computer to harm other people.
- Thou shalt not interfere with other people's computer work.
- Thou shalt not snoop around in other people's computer files.
- Thou shalt not use a computer to steal.
- Thou shalt not use a computer to bear false witness.
- Thou shalt not copy or use proprietary software for which you have not paid.
- Thou shalt not use other people's computer resources without authorisation or proper compensation.
- Thou shalt not appropriate other people's intellectual output.
- Thou shalt think about the social consequences of the program you are writing.

---

Further, there is more than one ethically defensible response (Ess, 2004; Ess and the AoIR, 2002). In particular, there are fundamental differences of approach to research ethics in the USA and European Union (EU) (Ess and the AoIR, 2002: 20). In the USA a utilitarian view of research ethics is held, while a deontological stance (human rights) view is held in member states of the EU (Capurro and Pringel, 2002: 193). In the former, the general view is that research can be carried out so long as, on balance, it does more good to society than harm, even if that involves breaching the privacy and anonymity of participants. In the latter, research must be eschewed if it risks causing any harm to participants. The problems are compounded by national legislation in many countries about the protection and use of electronic data. This varies from country to country and makes problematic which approaches to research ethics should be used when online interviews cross international boundaries.

## The Blurring of Public/Private Spaces

In online research, there is much debate about what constitutes private and public conversations. Some researchers see online texts as both publicly private and privately public (Waskul and Douglass, 1996). Others think that it depends on how individual participants in research projects perceive their communications with each other (Robson and Robson, 2002). 'The taken-for-granted boundaries of the public/private dichotomy [are being dissolved]' (Bowker and Tuffin, 2004: 231).

Online research gives rise to a number of issues around what constitutes public and private places and conversations in cyberspace (Sharf, 1999). Chat rooms and discussion forums can be viewed as both public and private spaces. The wide variety of sites makes a vast amount of data accessible for researchers to garner and interpret. Observing and analysing Internet artefacts already in the public domain such as Internet Home Pages can indicate a lot about individual or group identities and views (Walker, 2000). Linked to this, there is a huge amount of archived electronic data that is publicly available that do not require participant consent for access, although some participants may have an expectation of privacy (Walther, 2002).

Online spaces can be public and private simultaneously. Inviting participants to join a research project through a newsgroup or discussion forum, can be perceived as an invasion of private space because the posting is not perceived as relevant to the group's discussion. Ethical practice would be to approach the moderator of the chat room or news group but even then attempts to access them may be considered as spamming and not acceptable. Although an online discussion group might be accessible to the public the conversations taking place might be perceived as confidential by the participants.

Another component is the topics being discussed and the extent to which it represents personal information that individuals may not want to have shared in the public domain (Elgesem, 2002). There is a difference between information that is publicly *accessible* [sic] and that which is publicly *disseminated* [sic] (Fox and Roberts, 1999: 651, original emphasis), an issue we return to in Chapter 9.

For participants this makes it problematic to know to what extent they should divulge personal information because they are not sure to what extent that information will be broadcast in an even more public domain. It is for this reason that Ess and the AoIR (2002) argues that researchers are more likely to persuade participants to disclose personal information if they establish a safe online environment. However, in asynchronous focus group interviews using regular listserv or bulletin boards, the interaction will be less private and this may lead participants to be less candid than in email interviews.

This raises issues about how online data can be ethically collected and handled in research (Bakardjieva and Feenberg, 2000). Online data gathering can be disruptive and destroy the safety and security of belonging to an online group (Reid, 1996). However, some researchers regard online conversations to be in the public domain rather than as private conversations. This, they argue, allows them to gather these conversations as data without first gaining permission from the instigators of the conversations. Such activity is sometimes described as 'harvesting' and 'flies in the face of what thousands … of internet group members feel is permissible and ethical' (Sharf, 1999: 252).

Other researchers regard lurking as a legitimate means of discovering the focus of particular websites that they may want to research. Bakardjieva and Feenberg (2000) discuss the concerns they had in doing this when trying to choose sites to research. They recognised that although it was possible to access online sites easily, other participants on those sites did not know they were there or why they were there. The problem is compounded when researchers harvest extracts from conversations on sites when trying to decide which site to use for research. Conversely, consulting the members of an online community and gaining permission on each publicly accessible website that might provide a research site can take considerable time.

As participants of online research projects may consider their communications to be private, even if that privacy extends to the whole community (Gatson and Zweerink, 2004), so 'lurking' on discussion forums is of doubtful ethicality. It is akin to eavesdropping on conversations without first gaining permission from the other participants to do so (Bakardijeva and Feenberg, 2000; Coleman, 2006). King (1996) argues that all researchers should take seriously the level of perceived privacy that members of online communities attach to their communications and not lurk in any way, however justifiable the reasons for it when constructing research projects. NESH (2003) considers lurking unethical, and insist that Internet researchers should declare their presence and purpose when entering an online group.

### Gaining and Sustaining Informed Consent

Research is intended to be of reciprocal or mutual benefit to researchers, participants and society, not just a one-way arrangement. When negotiating entry into a research project, researchers should make clear to participants how they and other people might benefit from the research in which they are being invited to take part (Robson and Robson, 2002).

The grounds for informed consent in face-to-face research also apply to online environments (see Box 5.3) . So researchers need to gain participants' informed consent to take part in research from the beginning of a study, that is, from the time that they set up an online research project. They need to identify themselves and their purposes when they begin their studies. They also need to define what texts will be stored and saved, and in what way they will be stored and used. They will need to construct a means through which participants can check and confirm the meaning of their texts/speech acts before they are used outside the conversations of the project communities for which they were originally intended. Further, researchers will have to explain clearly to their putative participants how their identities and, possibly that of other participants in the online research project too, will be disguised to avoid the privacy of themselves and their correspondents being infringed.

To some extent the technology of the Internet facilitates the construction of voluntary participation by participants. However, gaining informed consent online can be more problematic as it can be easier for participants to deceive the researcher, as we discuss in the next chapter. The absence of the physical presence of a researcher seems to make it easier for some participants to commence their discussions, especially in synchronous online interviews where there is no moderator present. In asynchronous interviews, participants can respond as and when it suits them irrespective of reminders by researchers for responses because of the time lag. This 'silence' or lack of obvious signal by participants might also be interpreted as an indication that they are, perhaps temporarily, withdrawing their informed consent to participate. In such interviews the reasons for participants dropping-out of the research may not be transparent or open to investigation. Hodgson (2004) found this in her online interviews of participants' experiences of self-injury. This reiterates that informed consent is not something that is merely garnered at the start of a study but must be sustained throughout the study by empowering participants to feel comfortable to also withdraw consent.

One aspect of creating an ethical framework for communication online is by researchers and participants agreeing the nature and style of communication between them. Netiquette is an important help in clarifying this (Hall et al., 2004) and can prevent aggressive and insulting behaviour (Madge, 2006). It includes often unspoken rules about what is considered appropriate and polite and respectful behaviour online. Netiquette is inevitably flexible, as different types of online venues will have different rules and conventions depending on the nature of the online project and types of interviews being used.

Based on their research with newsgroups, Hall et al. (2004) identified a number of netiquette considerations (see Box 5.5). These provide a useful ethical framework that can be applied when constructing online research projects.

---

## Box 5.5    Netiquette guidelines for Internet researchers

(i) The subject header used in any posting must not misinform the participant nor create misunderstandings between the researcher and participants.

(ii) Self-identification and self-presentation of the researcher are critical, as receivers of the research will form their evaluations about the credibility of the research and the researcher – this is discussed in more detail in the next chapter.

(iii) To ensure respect for those being researched, the researcher must be familiar with the common language used by the participants, including jargon, abbreviations, acronyms, emoticons and common grammatical rules.

(iv) Researchers should always ask appropriate questions, and to do this researchers must acquaint themselves on the subject matter before asking for help.

(v) Prior understanding of the specific culture of the group/community should be attained by either observing the group for a period of time, or through a review of online FAQs and archives.

(vi) The researcher has an obligation to inform the participants about the purpose, nature, procedures and risks of the research. (Hall et al., 2004: 244–7)

---

To sustain the informed consent of participants, online researchers need to ensure that they have due regard for the cultures/communities/individuals with which and whom they are working. Further, researchers need to be able to inform participants of the processes of a project whenever participants request information about it. As we discuss in Chapter 9, establishing clear and ethical procedures for data collection and curation (ESRC, 2005: 7) helps to reassure participants that the risk of harm to them is minimised. Making clear the processes of dissemination helps participants to appreciate that the projects in which they are engaged are worthwhile and are intended to have some beneficial outcomes for society.

### Protecting Participants' Confidentiality, Privacy and Anonymity

Researchers working online face a variety of dilemmas to try to ensure their participants' privacy. Some of these reflect the particularities of research that might spread across cultural and political boundaries and have to meet the requirements of participants' different legal and cultural systems

(Ess and the AoIR, 2002: 3). In online research, expectations of privacy become complicated because different sites have differing expectations of the ways in which participants should interact. The site in which the research is conducted means researchers need to think about the implications of particular choices (Walford, 2006).

Such dilemmas reflect how online researchers approach their online interviews especially where participants may be vulnerable or the topic is sensitive. For example, if online researchers want to interview young people they need to think about the nature of the virtual environment (such as chat rooms that are extremely popular with young people), and whether they are most suited to their needs so as not to compromise research both legally and ethically (see Masson, 2005). Researchers need to ensure that arrangements for interviewing online are such that participants feel safe during the research and are not victimised. However, the faceless nature of the Internet raises questions about the identities of those engaged in the online interaction. Researchers need to gain appropriate consents from gatekeepers as well as the young people, establish clearly who they are and the purposes of their projects in terms that can be understood by the participants. Researchers cannot assume that young people have chosen to be online. Nor can they afford to compromise their research practice.

Protecting participants' privacy is a particular issue in online interviews that seek to gather sensitive data. The extent to which participants may be willing to be open and honest with researchers is likely to depend heavily on the extent to which the researchers can construct a secure environment for communication and one which protects participants' anonymity. This allows participants to feel confident that their privacy is protected and the risk of harm to them is minimised to a level acceptable to them (Clandinin and Connelly, 2000). Some of the participants in our studies revealed concerns about protecting their privacy and anonymity online especially as they were revealing personal (and sometimes sensitive) information about their professional lives (James and Busher, 2006).

Secure or private online environments pose less of a threat to participants' privacy than more open environments (Ess and the AoIR, 2002: 7). Where participants converse with researchers in a secure or private environment, for example a discussion board within a virtual learning environment (VLE), or a password-protected sector of a website, there is less likely to be a threat to their privacy and so less risk of harm to them than if they were engaged in a more open environment. The latter might be email, a public chat room or a blog (Ess and the AoIR, 2002: 7).

In the more open environments researchers need to take much greater care to protect the privacy of participants if they are to protect them from harm. For example, participants need to be made aware when their conversations are not taking place in a private setting (Barnes, 2004), so that they can make an informed choice about whether or not to participate. However this is similar to some onsite research when it is impossible to completely protect the privacy and anonymity of participants. For example, if a participant is one of only a few people in a particular field of activity or in an identifiable workplace, that person will remain partially visible no matter how careful researchers are (Walford, 2006).

In our studies, some of our participants' initial responses indicated their underlying fears that the email records of their conversations with us might make them visible. This was in spite of sending them the rubrics shown in Chapter 4 about how the email interviews would be carried out. They feared that the records of their conversations, no matter how carefully processed, would make their views instantly visible. In some macro-cultures, as discussed in Chapter 7, there is less concern to respect the privacy of online conversations than in others. Although the participants did not question our integrity as researchers and our efforts to safeguard confidentiality, it was only their prior knowledge of us face-to-face that gave them the confidence to continue with the research and give us their explicit informed consent. In our studies much depended on the personal relationships we had been or were able to develop with our participants that allowed them to trust us.

Researchers need to protect themselves from harm by verifying the trust-worthiness of a research project's data. This is problematic whether research is conducted online or face-to-face (Carter, 2005). In online research, participants and researchers are hidden from each other by the 'smoked mirror' of the Internet as a consequence of the visual anonymity and pseudonymity. These can disguise participants' identities and thus make it easier for people to play with their views and perspectives (Jacobson, 1999). Participants' presentation of self, whether playful, superficial, or written in an engaged way makes a considerable difference to the quality of a research project and the trustworthiness of its outcomes (James, 2003). However, it is the way in which participants' stories are constructed and the consistency with which they present themselves that provides the strongest reassurance to researchers of the trustworthiness of their accounts whether in online research or face-to-face research. Lee (2006) refers to this as patterned knowledge and recommends it as a source of establishing the trustworthiness of online accounts.

### Ethical Dilemmas in Publishing Research

The ethical issues and practical problems surrounding the curation and dissemination of online data are 'related to the special features of online communications' (Elgesem, 2002: 201). Records of participants' online conversations, even if carefully processed, can make participants' views instantly visible, because their email addresses contain part or all of their real names or their domains, making it possible in public sites to retrieve messages

(Eysenbach and Till, 2001). So the apparent privacy of individuals – they seem to be unseen to each other and the researchers – is instantly breached by some of the characteristics of online discussions. However, although certain elements of emails and other online postings, such as headers and signatures, appear to indicate the origin of a message, the real origin and, so, authorship of messages can be hidden with relatively ease (Lee, 2006).

Gaining permission to pass on/make use of personal stories or interviews to publish research from online communities can be difficult to obtain. Sharf (1999) joined an online community overtly and presented herself as a researcher from the start. While many members were in agreement with her wanting to draw on their stories to publish, because she had been an active member of the community, some were very doubtful about her wish.

There are many reasons why participants may be unhappy about their online texts/speech acts being used for purposes other than the online discussions for which they were originally constructed. First, many members of online communities believe that their communications are private dialogues, even when they are communicating to an internationally based community, so they are loath to have their perceived private conversations made public through the publication of research.

Second, the publication of people's conversations represents the appropriation of texts by researchers to use them for purposes other than that for which they were intended. This represents in some way the alienation of people from their own production (of text/speech acts) (Bakardjieva and Feenberg, 2000). People feel they have the right to decide what should be done with the property they have created.

Finally, people may be unwilling to have their text/speech acts appropriated by researchers. Participants in research projects may want to edit their conversations before they are published since they were not originally constructed for public display. Participants may be concerned about how they might (re)present themselves through the style and content of their text/speech acts. Or they may be concerned that there are details in them that might breach theirs or others privacy or confidentiality were they published in a public domain.

## Conclusion

The ethical challenges of online research are complex in part because participants can often inhabit several different time and space zones. The resolution of these complexities is far from simple given the various different stances to making ethical choices found in the USA, Europe and other parts of the world. There is currently no consensus among online researchers about how to deal with issues relating to public/private spaces, netiquette and informed consent, protecting privacy and anonymity and the trustworthiness of the data. The virtual and often anonymous nature of the Internet communication means that researchers must 'establish their bona fide status and the boundaries of the study more carefully than they might in a face-to-face situation' (Sanders, 2005: 78).

So every research project has to negotiate its own agreed norms between researchers and participants to establish an ethical framework of process. This negotiation is central to persuading participants that they are protected from intentional or unintentional harm and so free to (re)present themselves truthfully. Such a framework from the outset should include an 'ethics of care' that at the very least involves a respect for the interests and values of those who participate in online research (Capurro and Pringel, 2002: 194). It must also make clear whether or not the environment in which the discussions are conducted is secure so participants are aware of the risks they might be facing. Secure environments ensure that the risk to participants' privacy is minimised.

Participating in any research involves ethical risks to the individuals concerned. What is at issue is how those risks can be minimised by researchers. Hammersley (1998) commends a constantly reflective process by researchers on the rigorous standards of probity that are required as a safeguard. Further, participants must be helped to be fully aware of the risks involved so that they can freely choose whether or not they want to take part (Berger and Patchner, 1988). In seeking to protect participants from harm online research is no different from face-to-face research projects. 'What has become more difficult is determining how to ensure ethical use is made of texts, sounds and pictures that are accessed for study' (Jones, 2004: 179).

## Practical Tips for Online Researchers

- Establish your ethical stance as a researcher at the beginning of a project.
- Gain participants' informed consent to take part in research right from the beginning of a study, i.e. from the time that they join or the researcher sets up an online community of some sort.
- Identify who you are and the rationale for the research study.
- Define what texts will be stored and saved, and in what way they will be stored and used.
- Construct a means with participants through which members can check and confirm the meaning of their texts/speech acts before they are used outside the conversations of the communities for which they were originally intended.
- Explain clearly to putative participants how their identities, and possibly that of the online community too, will be disguised to avoid the privacy of themselves and their correspondents being infringed.
- Make clear to participants in online research how they and other people might benefit from the research in which they are being invited to take part.

- Use language that is of an appropriate level to participants whether for age or familiarity with English.
- Throughout a project, always be willing to respond to participants' ethical queries about the processes of the project, and do so promptly.

## Further Reading

Johns, M.D. Chen, S.L.S. and Hall G.J. (eds) (2004) *Online Social Research: Methods, Issues and Ethics*. Oxford: Peter Lang Publishing.

Busher, H. and James, N. (2007) 'Ethics of educational research: an agenda for discussion', in A. Briggs and M. Coleman (eds), *Research in Educational Management*, 2nd edn. London: Paul Chapman. pp. 106–22.

Madge, C. (2007) 'Developing a geographers' agenda for online research ethics', *Progress in Human Geography*, 31 (5): 654–74.

# SIX

## Constructing Credibility and Authenticity

Overview: this chapter explores the credibility and authenticity of data gathered using online interviews. It will discuss the implications of textual self-presentation for assuring the authenticity of research projects, and what leads researchers to accept participants' statements of identity at face value when they lack the information provided in face-to-face encounters. It also examines the debates around combining online and offline research and whether it is possible to get closer to social reality as a means of enhancing the rigour of the constructed method and the credibility of the data.

### Introduction

Chapter 4 explored how communication online is starkly dislocated in time and space. Derrida (in Wolfreys, 1998) points out that otherness (alterity) and identity are written in time and space. Writing is the process of inscribing identity. But this also contains the possibility of creating many identities which may be differentiated in different contexts. However, the identities that are inscribed are never complete but always immanent. So there is always the deferment of a completed definition of a person's identity (Derrida in Wolfreys, 1998). This affects the way that people can know each other especially in online conversations that are deprived of many normal interactive social processes.

When individuals interact online, particularly in virtual communities, it becomes possible to construct and affirm identities based on norms and beliefs that are personal yet supported by others. With the emergence of new technologies, such as blogs, Facebook and MySpace, different types of identities can be presented in distinct Internet environments (Kennedy, 2006). This raises questions about how people construct online identities and the extent to which they reveal their 'real' physical selves in such exchanges.

For researchers, knowing the identity of those with whom they communicate can aid in understanding and evaluating an interaction (Donarth, 2001). In the disembodied virtual world, identity can become ambiguous. This is the reason why some individuals seek participation and meaning online. For other individuals, it can connect them from diverse locations and facilitate the growth of meaningful communities and identities (Williams, 2006: 179). The conditions under which people self-disclose in such exchanges is a matter of considerable importance for online researchers (Lee, 2006). However, when participants are virtual, there are problems around how researchers can be assured about the credibility of the information that is transmitted online. Participants can choose to exploit the virtuality of the research site in order to experiment with the presentation of self.

A major debate in Internet research relates to the authenticity and trustworthiness of the data gathered (Carter, 2005). This has been to clarify whose voices are heard in textual self-presentation and how researchers establish that participants' voices reflect accurately the views they hold. This chapter explores the implications this has for constructing credible and authentic research online when all or part of the data is collected online. Part of that problem is what leads researchers to accept participants' statements of identity and take narratives at face value when they lack the information provided in face-to-face encounters. The chapter will also examine the debates around combining online and offline research, and whether it is possible to get closer to social reality as a means of enhancing the rigour of the constructed method and the credibility of the data.

## The Formation of 'Online' Identity in the Postmodern Age

Within the social sciences considerable attention has been given to the idea that virtual spaces can allow for the construction of new identities. Online interaction involves spaces as places where an individual can take on multiple identities in ways never before possible and bring about changes in conventional notions of identity itself (Turkle, 1995). This argument stems from Turkle's research that examined college students' experiences of MUDs. Many of her participants commented that a part of their identity only existed inside the MUD she was researching.

The ability to form multiple identities online has been indicative of a postmodern phenomenon – the fragmentation of the individual.

> The identities that emerge from these interactions – fragmented, complex, diffracted through the lenses of technology, culture and new technocultural formations – seem to be ... more visible as the critters we ourselves are in the process of becoming, here at the close of the mechanical age. (Stones, 1996: 36)

This suggests that in such anonymous environments, identity can be broken down into fragments. The online self can be viewed as multiple, transitory and always in the process of being constructed and reconstructed (Cavanagh, 2007), suggesting that:

> The interruptive practices associated with fluid identity relate to the construction of virtual space, where the fragmented self becomes dispersed, and that both make difficult the evolution of resilient online personae and communities. (Kolko and Reid, 1998: 218)

However, some online researchers have found that participants work to 'reincorporate their experiences of themselves and of others' selves into integrated, consistent wholes' (Kendall, 1999: 62). Identity then is not always fragmented but stable and unified. This stability is constructed through the ongoing dialogues and discourses emerging online. In understanding her participants' sense of self and the meanings they gave to their online participation, Kendal spent time with her participants to observe what they did online as well as what they said about what they did. In her study *Bluesky*, an important part of the interaction took place offline. This affected participants' interpretation of the online interaction as they sometimes tried to phone or write to other participants who had disappeared from the MUD for periods of time. The issue of the effects of offline contexts on participants' understandings of their online experiences will be explored in more depth later in the chapter.

What links the work of Turkle and Kendal is the way in which the virtual environment is seen as a site in which fragmented, postmodern identities are realised (Kennedy, 2006). 'The authentic self collapses into the presentation – or representation – of the self' (Walker, 2000: 100). This suggests a shifting and decentred postmodern self that has Internet freedom to present multiple identities that face-to-face interaction lacks in significant ways:

(i)   Individuals are dislocated from the online environment in both time and space.
(ii)  The lack of physical presence makes it difficult to verify misrepresentation and fabrication.
(iii) Identities can be recreated and reshaped.
(iv)  Identities can be under construction and thus beyond reproach.
(v)   Identities can be deleted if they do not live up to individuals' expectations.

However, the issue of multiplicity and authenticity in the presentation of self has been challenged. In a world of multiple selves can one identity be viewed as more superior than another? As one of Turkle's (1995: 14) participants comments '… why grant superior status to the self that has the body when the selves that don't have bodies are able to have different kinds of experiences'. Individuals cannot create selves that are distinct from their historical lived experiences, but they can construct different personae in professional or personal circumstances. Although fragmented, these personae can become an integral part of the self.

The Internet facilitates the fragmentation of the self, but it also exaggerates the possibilities for individuals to experiment with different forms of presentations of self unhindered (Walker, 2000). Yet in face-to-face encounters, it is not possible to physically isolate our social faces as we 'all inhabit the same space and are identified as one person by those around us' (Kolko and Reid, 1998: 219).

The experiential dimension of online interaction suggests that participants' claims to online selves and online communities should be perceived as existing through the same processes of interaction by which any self and community emerge, are maintained, and are transformed in everyday life. (Waskul and Douglass, 1997: 379)

By the end of the first decade of the 21st century, virtual reality environments have developed to the point that '... postmodern identity play' has moved towards 'the equally postmodern, dynamic of hyper-identity' in which identity is located as a product of group membership (Cavanagh, 2007: 124). Cavanagh uses the example of a blog to highlight how 'one's identity emerges from whom one knows and one's associations and connections' (Turkle, 1995: 258). This suggests that identity formation can be a product of online membership. Yet individuals have to be part of a context in which they can identify with others and be identified (Waskul and Douglass, 1997). This illustrates the social constructed nature of the online environment that contains shared understandings and information:

... there is one thing we can be entirely certain: that there is somebody, somewhere, at this very moment, exchanging ... messages with you, otherwise this interaction could not be taking place ... (Slater, 2002: 232)

## How Do Participants See Themselves? Performance and Presentation Online

The social construction of self is important to understanding the processes of online qualitative research. Until the spread of the Internet in the 1990s most discussions about how people constructed themselves and presented themselves socially focused on how this was done within the confines of physical and social contacts with other people. Goffman (1959: 13) prefaces his discussion by establishing the context for them of individuals in the (physical) presence of other people. Within these contexts people deliberately give signals and unintentional signals to observers of their actions. On the Internet, however, many of the unintentional signals can be masked even if many personal signifiers still tend to build up a coherent pattern that makes a person identifiable (Lee, 2006).

So people can still construct multiple realities for themselves within the various social contexts and communities they inhabit (Berger and Luckman, 1966; Zhao, 2006). However, there may be strong similarities between the marginally varying identities that people construct to represent their essential selves (Giddens, 1991). Such identities are socially constructed through the range of experiences people encounter and are never complete (Derrida in Wolfreys, 1998).

As discussed in Chapter 4, in the Internet age, the construction by people of their senses of reality and of themselves can no longer be bounded merely by their physical presence in time and space. It has become difficult to ignore the ways in which people construct self and their understandings of reality in the interstices of physical space and the spatial/time attenuations of the Internet.

Similarly too, when the Internet is used for the collection of interview data, it can provide a site in which research participants can construct their identities using a variety of techniques to present themselves online. The distance between body and performance online means that it does become difficult for researchers to authenticate the claims that participants make about themselves. The scope for participants to control the presentation of the self increases, leading to both the production and disclosure of new online personae, as well as those that can be concealed (Mann and Stewart, 2000). This raises issues about the nature of 'performance' that can take place online, in terms of how both participants and researchers can 'play' with their identity in the social space (Hardey, 2004). The opportunities for experimenting with self-presentation are a deliberate feature of some virtual worlds. Participants may choose to negotiate the boundary between the private and the public in online self-presentation using a range of strategies (see Box 6.1).

---

## Box 6.1   Experimenting with self-presentation in online interviews

- Through disembodiment and anonymity participants take on many new identities that may have little connection to their offline selves.
- Identity information, such as pseudonyms can be created.
- Individuals can become identified with a nickname that promotes a particular image or mask that can hide and unveil identities or become a badge of identity.
- Participants can (re)construct playful identities in which they become unaccountable for their online personae.
- The ability for participants to mask their identity may lead them to be more active in voicing or disclosing their opinions.
- Participants can build identity knowledge and interpret the social characteristics of the other, either verbally or non-verbally. This can be more actively pursued through identity cues.

---

Such experimentation has a number of implications for assuring research authenticity in online interviews. It can become difficult to ascertain the person who is behind the name. This presents further dilemmas about how possible it is to trust anything that the individual claims to be (Slater, 2002). Researchers should not be surprised to find that online '… people bring place and identity with them as they simultaneously find themselves in a new space in which they are creating … perhaps new identities' (Gatson and Zweerink, 2004: 185).

Bodily presence in a face-to-face interview can signify mutuality, commitment and trust through a sense of shared purpose (Seymour, 2001). However, in the online interview this bodily presence is removed. Further, outward acts of movement, posture and emotional expression that are important elements in determining how individuals see themselves and how they are perceived by others are also invisible as illustrated in the following vignette.

### Vignette: The presentation of self in an email interview

In the study of James (2003) (see Chapter 3 for a detailed outline), she had to deal with how her participants would engage in the presentation of self in the absence of non-verbal communication such as gesture, tone of voice and facial expressions. As the interviews progressed she found that her research participants began to take greater ownership of the processes of narrative construction as their online life stories began to unfold. She found that the 'lived body' was invisible during the interview. Yet the mannered behaviours, pre-interpreted meanings and unstated assumptions were clearly 'visible' during the online interviews. In turn, this influenced the nature of the participants' online narratives and the construction of their identities. They located themselves and their biographies in a context, arranging the details of their biographies into an identity 'repertoire' (Walker, 2000: 105) which allowed the researcher to see and react to this presentation. In effect, the participants were 'telling' their stories in ways that anchored their identity on the Internet. They also represented an ongoing reflexive process, as evident in this participant's comment:

> ... this process has made me wonder where it [identity] came from originally ... and surprised me how much my identity ... as a psychologist/researcher influences the way I conduct my current professional duties ... My involvement therefore has been a reflexive one, especially in the times I have been answering your questions and I was able to answer them once I'd given thought to what I wanted to say – there is not much time to reflect otherwise. (James, 2007: 968)

Yet, a disembodied online interaction can also encourage individuals to disclose. In Kanayama's (2003) online study of Japanese elderly people, the participants did not mask their identities and become someone else. The participants' disclosure was really important in the process of constructing relationships online. They actively engendered identifiable personalities through naming themselves or disclosing personal information. This in turn created an informal interviewing atmosphere. In presenting the self online, the absence of bodily presence for these participants, as well as outward acts of movement, posture and emotional expression were important as they felt free from perceptions of age and gender that often limited their contact with others.

## Authenticating Online Identities Through Offline Contexts?

In online research interviews, the existence of the participants and researcher within the research context is reliant on text (Markham, 2004a: 339). Identities can be negotiated and reproduced and indexed in a variety of ways (Wilson and Peterson, 2002). Individuals can express themselves in ways that are different from everyday life, allowing improvisation and word play to flourish (Danet, 1998). Of course, there is no guarantee that such identity performances will not occur in offline environments. As Derrida (in Wolfreys, 1998) argues, speech is as much a form of constructed text as is writing. It is also intimately connected with the performance and (re)presentation of identity in particular contexts. So, as in everyday life, whether face-to-face or online, individuals will review and rewrite their histories and perspectives in the light of developing experiences. As will be discussed in more detail in Chapter 8, the emergence of patterns of interactivity and narrative by and between participants online can help to build confidence in the projected identities of participants in their online texts.

Identity play is a well-established phenomenon that pre-dates the advent of the Internet. Individuals have always engaged in different presentations of self, and did so before the existence of the virtual world (Kendall, 1999). Further, Internet users generally do produce relatively consistent performances of their identities online (Hine, 2000: 119). However, researchers will hold up the textual representation of the participants next to their physical personae to add credibility to research findings (Markham, 2004b).

In the offline world the presentation of self is based not only on what individuals choose to show, for example through gesture or tone of voice, but how that is perceived by others in the space of social interaction (Matthews, 2006). What participants write about themselves online may also be shaped by their perceptions, and the likely reactions of the researcher to what they say. This suggests that what participants write is not necessarily a reflection of how they see themselves (Hammersley and Treseder, 2007). In such circumstances, the researcher may need to test what is authentic against regular patterns of interaction in their online research (Mann and Stewart, 2000: 211).

Some researchers have addressed this issue by meeting participants offline to triangulate findings and add authenticity. They take the view that online interactions are deeply embedded in and shaped by offline situations and relationships (Xie, 2006). Early research by Correll (1995) found that when she met her participants face-to-face she was able to verify some of the things that they had said online about their offline experiences. James (2007) too found this in her online study of academic identities. In her email interviews, some participants' responses were superficial and playful. It was evident that they did not always want 'to participate in substantive discussion' (Gaiser, 1997: 142).

By interviewing the participants offline she added authenticity to their descriptions of how they saw themselves, as well as depth to her interpretations of their identities.

Some offline relationships are constructed in the course of normal professional exchanges. In these circumstances, researchers can use the pre-existing relationships to further discuss the issues raised online (Busher, 2001; James, 2003). This need not necessarily be done through a face-to-face interview. Instead, opportune moments can be taken to 'progressively embody the other' (Slater, 2002: 241). This approach allows researchers to make more use of the body visible (voice, gesture, tone). In this sense the virtual world and the real world merge, drawing the researcher and participants together to interact. Rich and meaningful research relationships develop both visually and online through their textual self-presentation. This level of self-exposure can reinforce the participants' authentic expressions of self as they return to the online interviews (James, 2007: 971).

Adopting this approach reinforces how the construction and understanding of online texts can be shaped by the nature of participant and researcher interactions that transcend both online and offline boundaries (James and Busher, 2006). The prior knowledge of participants can help to verify their identities, or to cross-reference their views and perspectives. This can be done through normal processes of triangulation, by observing and participating in the social situations which are being explored. In addition, the researchers' investment in the research relationship – the mutual disclosure and repeated interactions, means they can be reassured about the authenticity of the participants' written texts. In these contexts, it is possible to get a sense of who is online, who the participants really are and the trustworthiness of what has been written (Giese, 1998).

Nevertheless, other researchers argue that online discourses and identities are valid in themselves and do not need to be verified offline (Hine, 2000). Individuals do not leave the body, and all its material inequalities behind when they enter cyberspace (O'Connor and Madge, 2003). It is the embodied participant who interacts online, and they can never escape from lived experiences (Jones, 1999). Identity construction includes dimensions of complexity and fluidity that can characterise both participants and researcher. Gatson and Zweerink (2004) found that the identities portrayed by their participants emphasised the importance of discourse and experience in shaping both the real and virtual worlds. Participants can simultaneously inhabit both online and offline environments (Turkle, 1995). Identities are inextricably linked with who people are, their commitments and values and are 'integral and continuous' (Kendall, 1999: 61). Processes of reflection on identity do not only happen in interviews and online exchanges. They happen in everyday life too, as individuals review and rewrite their histories and perspectives in the light of their developing experiences (James and

Busher, 2006). 'For this reason it is seen to be difficult to sustain a persona which is quite divorced from the "real" self' (Mann and Stewart, 2000: 210). The complexity of self, identity and perspective occurs face-to-face as well as online and affects how participants present themselves in conversations and actions in the conduct of research.

### Authenticating Online Data

The authenticity of data collected in the online environment is no more problematic than in any other. However, researchers should not 'bring some external criterion for judging whether it is safe to believe what informants say, but rather to come to understand how it is that informants judge authenticity' (Hine, 2000: 49) One approach is to ensure that the verification of online data as 'authentic' is an ongoing reflexive process that is 'situationally negotiated, rather than an objectifying process to be undertaken only when analysing the data themselves' (Carter 2005: 151).

In this approach, disembodiment and anonymity of online interactions can serve as 'a foundation for the building of trust and establishing real world relationships rather than the construction of fantasy selves' (Hardey, 2002: 579). In the disembodied environment, researchers can be more assured about the authenticity of the interview data. In particular, asynchronous interviews allow participants the time to reflect on their responses. They can avoid unwelcome self-exposure that they could risk in the ad hoc self-presentation that is possible face-to-face (Mann and Stewart, 2000). Participants too can reveal their identity statements, and actively seek to gain identity knowledge of the researcher by sharing viewpoints. By working hard to develop research relationships online, researchers can gauge the sincerity, authenticity and individuality of the disembodied research participants (James and Busher, 2006).

In asynchronous interviews, part of the process of helping to construct authentic voices, is by allowing participants to take greater ownership of the construction of their texts so that their voice comes through. By letting participants own the construction of the culture of the interviews, researchers not only establish participants' consent to be part of a study, but also produce more reflexive data. Adopting this approach can open up possibilities for participants to respond to others' identity play and engage in constructing identity knowledge about each other (Lee, 2006). It can also present opportunities for both researcher and participants to better understand how they each come to shape their identities. James (2007) invested her own identity into the research relationship as an attempt to democratise narrative exchanges, to have a more equal interaction and a dialectical relationship (Illingworth, 2001). She eventually took on a different role as a 'participant researcher' (Seymour, 2001) (see Box 6.2).

James (2007) found that by self-disclosing, she was better placed to judge the sincerity and authenticity of her participants' narratives. The sharing of personal experiences  played a significant  role in enhancing mutual understandings of both the researcher's and participant's identity.  Further, by the researcher talking about herself, and through encouraging her participants to do the same, such self-disclosure can 'alleviate the harm of unaccountability and deceptiveness of what is said in disembodied on-line interaction' (Lee, 2006: 17).

P:   ... My experiences as an academic psychologist have shaped my professional identity in that I am acutely aware of the rigour with which research is carried out and so feel able to lend some authority to observations/judgments based on the robustness of empirical inquiry ...

R:   I think that's interesting. In considering the issue myself I have found that my professional identity is linked not only to the working context and the culture within which I work but other identities, which are important to me ... These identities merge with each other and are influenced by each other in terms of how I live my life as a whole ...

P:   I absolutely agree with you. For instance, I teach gender and Psychology and regard myself as a feminist, so this has a bearing on how I deliver psychological material and how I am perceived. Similarly I am a parent so when talking about socialisation I feel I can lend some credibility from my own experience. My professional identity is completely bound up with my personality ... (James, 2007: 970)

The intense sharing of experiences can replace the interpersonal interaction that is the basis of face-to-face interactions (Walker, 2000). Thus in online interviewing it is possible to create trust in the participant's presentation of self without the usual interactional cues to authenticate the identity presented. Disembodiment therefore does not have to result in interview data that is dishonest and fraudulent. Researchers can become more assured about the authenticity and credibility of their participants in online interviews, and what they disclose when there is a commonality of identities and self exposure between the researcher and participant (James and Busher, 2007). This can strengthen the claims of the study to be authentic as researchers 'learn to interpret participants' identity performances in the same way that participants themselves do (Kendall, 1999: 70). As explored in Chapter 8, trust can develop over time as individuals become familiar with one another (Whitty, 2002). When, researcher and participants do not share such commonalities, the researcher will need to spend time investing in the online interaction.

However, in synchronous group interaction, which is frequently a one-off occurrence, authenticity is more difficult (Mann and Stewart, 2000). Participants in online discussion forums may carefully manipulate the presentations of their discussions. Methodologically, as noted in Chapter 3, this raises questions about the 'act of identification' (LeBesco, 2004) which can distort communications in online settings. A stranger wanting to do academic research into online groups/communities will not always be welcomed and may be seen as an intruder (Paccagnella, 1997). Depending on the online context, participants may choose to become anonymous and to modify their presentation of self to meet the demands of the situation. Some participants have the option of negotiating 'actual social identities' in the non-verifiable presentation of an online 'virtual social identity' (Waskul and Douglass, 1997: 394).

Researchers who conduct synchronous interviews therefore have to decide whether they announce their research identities and presence as researchers or adopt a more naturalistic mode (Fox and Roberts, 1999). This choice may be easier where there is a commonality of identity. In O'Connor and Madge's (2003) 'cyberparents' research the participants and researchers shared identities as new mothers. This helped to facilitate synchronous online interviews. They found that they did not need to develop radically new ways of building rapport with their participants. Further, they posted photographs of themselves and shared their interests with the participants, giving distinct clues to their bodily identities.

In such contexts, the performance of identity requires the real physical presence of actual bodies at the same moment in time, and that once these bodies leave, nothing remains (Slater, 2002). Suddenly identity claims become unverifiable. When identity clues are missing, researchers need to get to know and understand the particular norms and values of the group/community in order to build trust. In doing so they can learn to interpret 'participants' identity performance' rather than briefly visiting the forum to generate research data (Kendall, 1999: 70). The experientially based knowledge of the participants may then become more significant than personal identity and enough to bolster the authenticity claims of the text (O'Connor and Madge, 2003).

## Conclusion

The tension between online and offline identities and environments reflects broader and well-established debates about authenticity and credibility within research using qualitative methods of inquiry. Nonetheless, when conducting interviews online, researchers must develop a sense about the truthfulness and candour of their participants as they would do in face-to-face interviews.

A number of researchers have tried to establish participant identity by combining both online and offline contexts to triangulate the findings. This has served as part of their reassurance regarding the authenticity and credibility of participants' discourses and interactions. In James's (2003, 2007) and Busher's (2001) studies, the best guarantee of authenticity was the way in which the participants' stories were closely aligned with their selves and identities, and the way in which the researchers tried to generate an open and honest dialogue with them. Yet, researchers have to recognise that whilst the stories that their participants write are grounded in their everyday lives, the written texts can still lead to the creation of a personae that bears little relationship to the participant's 'interactional self' in everyday 'non-screen life' (Denzin, 1999: 114). This raises a further question as to whether researchers should ascribe purpose and motive to the participants' lives without a knowledge of their offline lives.

One way forward is for researchers not to always assume that triangulating online research with offline contexts and face-to-face interactions will ensure truthfulness and candour. Instead they can accept participants' online interactions and discourses as a commitment to 'an authentic experience of self' (Lee, 2006: 20) as other Internet users would do (Hine, 2000). Researchers too can encourage participants to take greater ownership of discourses as they reflect their views. This makes the accurate presentation of their selves a shared responsibility with the researchers. In developing this complicity, participants can become responsible for the cultural reproduction of a research study, in which they have a part (James and Busher, 2007). They can have a stronger investment in ensuring that the outcomes of that study are credible and authentic. As the authors of the discourses, participants can and should be the authority that determines its authenticity and credibility.

## Practical Tips for Online Researchers

- Consider how, as researchers, we come to know our participants both online and offline.
- Do not assume that offline interactions will reveal more authentic data than that generated by online interactions.
- Combining online and offline interviews depends on the purposes of the research project as well as the characteristics of your participants' lives.
- Think about what is lost/gained in the move from online to offline interactions, and vice versa.
- Building relationships with participants online can generate an authentic dialogue.
- Allow your participants to shape the process and direction of the online interview thus aiding authenticity and credibility.
- Online and offline interviews can present different types of discourses and need to be carefully analysed.

### Further Reading

Hammersley, M. and Treseder, P. (2007) 'Identity as an analytic problem: who's who in 'pro-ana' websites?', *Qualitative Research*, 7 (3): 283–300.

Orgad, S. (2005) 'From online to offline and back: moving from online to offline relationships with research informants', in C. Hine (ed.), *Virtual Methods: Issues in Social Research on the Internet*. Oxford: Berg. pp. 51–66.

Rybas, N. and Gajjala, R. (2007) 'Developing cyberethnographic research methods for understanding digitally mediated identities', *Forum: Qualitative Social Research*, 8 (3): Art. 35. Available at: http://www.qualitative-research.net/fqs-texte/3-07/07-3-35-e. htm. Accessed 10 December 2007.

# SEVEN

## Issues of Inequality and Power Relations

Overview: this chapter examines the power relations and inequalities that exist between researchers and participants in online research projects. In particular, it explores how, in the faceless context of the Internet, individuals assert and protect their agency and identity from positions of remoteness. This includes considering the impact of new technologies and the cultures associated with them on social processes, such as processes of work and the construction of people's identities and the cultural and political environments in which people work. The inherent inequalities of power in research projects have important implications for how researchers construct their online interviews, and the ways in which researchers have to approach and work with potential online participants in their studies.

### Introduction

Online communication pervades every aspect of our lives. In part this is because the neo-liberal economic agenda has seized upon the Internet as a means of increasing global production to the benefit of some parts of the world, especially the West (Evans, 2004). This globalisation of production and consumption can be construed as a form of economic imperialism sponsored by the financial rationalism of the IMF and the World Bank (Bourdieu, 1998: 19).

The widespread use of online communication in professional and managerial workplaces, especially in technologically advanced countries, has increased the speed and volume of communication and intensified working practices. Individuals are often on the receiving end of a broader range of online communications than they need or want. The systems within which people work and with which they have to interact and struggle can limit their power to express themselves. People's lack of control over the text they receive via email can create a sense of disempowerment. It can seem to Internet users that they have no influence over the social rules that govern who is sent information about what regardless of whether or not the recipients want it (Sharf, 1999). This can be due to state surveillance as discussed later, or insecure websites and Internet connections (Joinson, 2005). It can also be linked to lack of technical knowledge to control online communications. For example, people may not understand the rules that govern website construction and use.

This chapter examines how power flows in the social and cultural environments in which people construct online conversations and social interactions. It examines how this can have a major influence on the ways in which people participate in online research projects, and how constructions of conversations and other social interactions through the Internet allow power to flow in various ways. In particular it explores how, in the anonymous context of the Internet, participants assert and protect their agency and identity from positions of remoteness. The last is affected by participants' perceptions of the (in)security of the electronic environment in which they work, itself a cultural construct. These issues have important implications for the ways in which researchers approach and work with potential online participants in their studies.

In discussing communication and power in online research it is important to locate it an understanding of power. This is discussed in Box 7.1.

---

### Box 7.1 A brief disquisition on power

People project power to assert their preferred values and choices over those of other people. This is a normal and legitimate part of the processes of institutions whether carried out by people holding senior positions or more junior ones hierarchically. People also use power to prevent other people making choices or, indeed, challenging the choices which have already been implemented, perhaps by trying to control the agenda for discussion (Lukes, 1974). All processes in formal organisations or informal social processes are negotiative, i.e. they involve politics as different people try to construct their agenda over or with others (Ball, 1987). So the construction of a research project involves the use of power and negotiation by its researchers and other participants to achieve an outcome.

The term 'power' in this chapter is used to cover both legitimate and formal uses of power, often described as 'authority', as well as personal sources of power and influence (Busher, 2006). It also indicates where and why people may lack power/suffer disempowerment and what they might try to do to rectify this in some circumstances. The use of authority and personal influence constitute legitimate processes which people use in a wide variety of formal and informal social processes, including those of research projects, to shape decisions (Ball, 1987). Power flows through processes of social interaction (Foucault, 1994) rather than being a resource that people exchange (Parsons, 1986), but exchange, whether physical or symbolic, time-lapsed, coterminous or contingent, is one of the conduits through which social, emotional, intellectual, physical and legal power flows in social interactions.

Power is not, therefore, an item that can be picked off a shelf. Power cannot be accessed or projected unless people engage in dialogue and action with other people and/or with social and organisational systems constructed by

---

people singly or in groups that can bestow authority on others who are chosen to act in its name. Interaction may be dispositional and latent but if there is none, whether face-to-face or at a distance, there is no flow of power.

Power is often perceived as having two main forms, that of authority arising from the offices which people hold in a formal organisation and that arising from influence (Bacharach and Lawler, 1980). The latter is said to come from people's personal and professional skills and knowledge. French and Raven (1968) suggest five different sources of power: physical power; control of resources; organisational or social position; expertise; personal magnetism – which might be considered akin to the notion of 'charisma' (Weber, 1947). Bennett (2001) offers two other sources of power: administrative/technical knowledge and the capacity to define norms of socially acceptable action. Torres (1999: 99) suggests there are five sources of power: 'physical force, the basis of coercion; control of necessary material resources, the basis for domination; the strength of the better argument, the basis for influence; the capacity to deliberately misrepresent, the basis for manipulation; and advantageous location within a system of meanings, the basis of authority.'

## Communication and Power Inequalities on the Internet

The invasion of the privacy of communications, especially online communications, has been compounded by societal cultures of surveillance that have been developed in many Western countries in response to the perceived enhanced threat of terrorism since 2001. Powerful world states have attempted to ensure the safety of the supply of raw materials for their industry and commerce by developing neo-colonial economic practices that project their power through globalisation (Evans, 2004).

The claimed heightened threat of terrorism in some Western countries has given rise to governments, quasi-governmental organisations and employers justifying monitoring citizens'/employees' email and Internet connections to find out if they are linked with potential terrorist activity (Coleman, 2006). Such actions or suspicion of such actions are likely to make people cautious about engaging in online communication for fear of having their privacy invaded or their economic or personal safety compromised. This intercept activity is in violation of the International Bill of Rights (Universal Declaration of Human Rights; International Covenant on Human Rights) promulgated by the United Nations and supported by 151/189 member states in 2003 (Coleman, 2006: 21). The Bill is intended to guarantee people's privacy, including protecting them from having their correspondence spied on. It is supposed to ensure that only designated legal or legalised state authorities are given the right to the surveillance of people's actions within a pre-existing legal framework.

In delineating who may have authority (legitimate power) to monitor other people's communications, the International Bill of Rights raises questions about the ethics of research. 'Lurking' on newsgroups and online communities is an invasion of privacy. It is an illegitimate use of power to survey people's activities through technological means without first gaining their permission. Even if the action is for utilitarian and potentially socially beneficial purposes, such as to explore the viability of a site for research (Bakardjieva and Feenberg, 2000), it still breaches the terms of the Bill of Rights. Some researchers overcome this dilemma by gaining post hoc permission from an online community to carry out research, after initially 'lurking' on a site. This approach acknowledges that covert research 'violates the principles of informed consent and may invade the privacy of those being studied' (BSA, 2002: para. 32) while legitimising this use of power by researchers in tightly circumscribed circumstances.

The online researcher cannot assume that participants have the freedom to speak freely on the Internet. Nor may there be any widely supported norms in many countries about how people's communications on the Internet might be used by third parties. This has implications for the viability of online research for many countries (Madge, 2006). In some non-Western countries, governments routinely carry out surveillance of Internet activities, such as in the Gulf States and China. This is to prevent citizens having access to websites or news that might carry information or views attacking the government. In Western societies, too, censorship and surveillance is evident. For example, the Australian government now requires ISPs to implement a mandatory Internet filtering/blocking system, which limits the availability of content to people. The US central government has severely restricted online speech using Internet filters or blocking software (Hessler et al., 2003). However, total censorship of information on the Internet is very difficult to achieve due to the underlying distributed technology of the Internet. Pseudonymity and data portals (such as Freenet) can allow unconditional free speech, as the technology guarantees that material cannot be removed and it is impossible to link the author of any information to a physical identity or organisation.

The facelessness of the Internet can encourage people to become more conformist to populist norms of Internet communication, usually policing their own actions (Foucault, 1977). This is in response to the gaze that is apparently thrown on people's actions by the disciplinary discourses emanating from the media. The media play an important part in promoting social norms but casting them in such ways that to dissent seems to be old fashioned, not progressive (Bourdieu, 1998).

As a consequence of the shift in cultural norms and expectations, people tend to respond to electronic communications more quickly than when communication is by hard copy or telephone. Participants (as suppliers) should be responsive to senders' (as consumers') demands regardless of what they are doing or in which time/space zone they inhabit. Dominant groups or people in societies and organisations assert cultural norms as a soft means of controlling people's behaviour (Lenski, 1986). This unobtrusive use of power allows the powerful to endow their actions or proposed actions with legitimacy in the eyes of subordinate others (Hardy, 1985: 390).

Despite the global reach of the Internet, different people in different societies have different levels of access to it because they lack computer hardware and software, and/or technical and literacy skills (Janelle and Hodges, 2000). People who are without access to online communications often are disadvantaged economically and not sure how to secure access to them (Evans, 2004). Hence, online research is more difficult in some parts of the world and certain social groups in every society are 'less connected' than others. It raises uncomfortable questions for online researchers about the construction of representative samples, and the extent to which certain voices in society are further marginalised by having insufficient access to Internet technologies.

If the new communications technologies threaten to disempower people in various ways, they also offer opportunities for people to assert their identities differently. In engaging with the new systems of communication and understanding how to manipulate its rules, people are able to assert their agency to reconstruct their identities in new ways (Giddens, 1991, 1984). This is discussed more fully in Chapter 6. Further, people with easy access to computers now have greater opportunities for communicating with each other and with a wide range of resources, enhancing their power to project themselves and their interests. Online communities, news groups and listserv offer a range of sites through which people can communicate professionally and socially, including opportunities for professional development, teaching and assessment (Reed, 2004). In turn these offer fascinating sites and foci for researchers interested in undertaking qualitative online research projects in real-time, or through asynchronous communications (Hine, 2000).

## Power Inequalities in Online Research

The political environments in which people work have a major influence on the ways in which people can participate in research projects. Online discourses and practices usually continue to reflect and reinforce the unequal power relations present in onsite institutions and social conventions (Madge and O'Connor, 2005). The anonymity of the Internet does not assuage them. Indeed it risks enhancing them. International participants in research projects will have to meet the requirements of their legal and cultural systems, which may be different from those of the researchers (Ess and the AoIR, 2002: 3).

This raises several questions for the online researcher about how to communicate across different cultural perspectives when conducting online interviews. Obtaining data about someone's life through online communication may seem easy and convenient, but it can also be a hazardous and uncertain procedure for both researcher and participants (Paccagnella, 1997). Insecure websites contribute to people's sense of insecurity for their privacy, confidentiality and anonymity. This represents a loss of power and control of communications by people, giving them an experience of alienation (Bakardjieva and Feenberg, 2000). People lose control over their production of cultural artefacts, in this case the text/speech acts of online communications. Although researchers try to limit the risks of this loss of control by agreeing with participants how their text/speech acts might be used in the research project, open access websites can be grazed by anybody who wants to log on.

To protect themselves against such loss of power (control) people may hesitate to engage in online interviews, especially with strangers or relatively unknown people, such as researchers inviting them to take part in projects. This sometimes makes it difficult for researchers to gain permission to carry out interviews with individuals online, or from online settings with groups (Bakardjieva and Feenberg, 2000). This is because putative participants have their own agenda when joining a research project. For example, they are likely to want to protect their privacy and the confidentiality of their views.

The extent to which participants are willing to be open and honest with researchers will depend upon their perception of the online research site which researchers construct. Where researchers construct a safe environment for the research, participants are likely to be willing to engage in meaningful conversations with each other and/or with researchers (Joinson, 2001). Without a safe environment, participants might fear they are at risk of flaming and receiving negative feedback (Smith, 2001), or at risk of having their actions viewed by lurkers with whom they might prefer not to communicate.

Alternatively, to protect their identities, members of online communities may prefer to adopt persona or masks behind which to hide (Kearney, 2003). The faceless nature of the Internet means that in some forms of online research, such as in chat rooms, participants may use pseudonyms. This is to protect their identity when discussing personal and sensitive topics (Hessler et al., 2003). The nature of the Internet can also help participants to protect their identity, even if some of the technical features of Internet communication help to indicate who the communicators might be (Lee, 2006).

The medium of online communications challenges users of the Internet to find ways of knowing and engaging authentically with their interlocutors other than those used in face-to-face communications. This is because of the lack of non-verbal cues of interpersonal/social interaction in online communication. Instead it is stripped down to text/speech acts that can be shown on a screen as a result of tapping a keyboard. So people cannot be sure to whom they are talking/writing and what social situations they are occupying contemporaneously, or were occupying when they wrote their text/speech act. This is not, however, to argue that social performance in online spaces takes place in a social vacuum. It is embodied in a Foucauldian sense (Foucault, 1977) even if that embodiment is only through the synapses of people's brains rather than through the brawn of their corporeal selves.

The invisibility of people in online communications also poses a threat to participants in online interviews. It is likely to lead to them understanding only crudely the habitus (Bourdieu, 1990) of other online participants in their different environments, as has been discussed in Chapter 4. Such understandings may be provisional, always in a process of becoming (Rodgers, 2004), and changing as the actors' relationships alter in the multiple contexts which they inhabit. However, it can lead to people communicating with other participants in an inappropriate manner. Developing literacies in making sense of social situations is an important skill for people entering any community, whether or not it is online (Bourdieu et al., 1994). One aspect of this is developing trust in their communicators through engaging with them (Lee, 2006). This is also discussed more fully in Chapter 8. As people become more skilled in their online performances, whether of reading online text/speech acts or of communicating their views, they become better able to interpret the situations in which they find themselves. It also allows them to become more skilled in asserting their views appropriately in online interactions, that is, to project power (Foucault, 1994) as well as to resist that of others.

Online communication is a potentially risky enterprise for many people. It can diminish people's sense of self-esteem, weakening their positive sense of identity (Giddens, 1991; Kearney, 2003). Further, people's ability to use language skilfully is an essential element in their power to engage in online discussions. Berger and Luckmann (1966, in Zhao 2006) point out the centrality of language to people's construction of knowledge and presentation of self. Moreover, online communication in research is predominantly carried out in English at present. This form of linguistic colonialism limits the power of people who do not speak English as a first language to express their views (Madge, 2006). This challenge to participants is compounded because, 'most research on the Internet is centred in Anglo-American cultural contexts' (Jankowski and van Selm, 2005: 203).

In online research interviews, then, non-native speakers of English might feel particularly threatened. They have to become adept at expressing themselves about sensitive personal topics and feelings in a language that is not their own. The lack of visual and non-verbal cues in online communication further limits their power to express themselves. Understandably, such circumstances may lead to participants withdrawing from research projects or reverting to text discussions in their native language. Both happened in a study of inclusive schools in greater Beirut (Bahous et al., 2006) (see Box 7.2).

---

## Box 7.2 Language and power in online interviews

A study of four elementary schools in Greater Beirut investigated why some schools, even when they are serving socially disadvantaged communities, seemed to be successful in fostering inclusion in education and student engagement with learning.

Its key questions focused on what cultures were constructed in some schools serving children from relatively disadvantaged social communities and in what ways these reflected an inclusion agenda; how these cultures were manifested in the teaching and learning process and in the relationships established between teachers, students and parents; and what evidence there was that students and teachers might be excited to work in this culture/school and parents be excited to work with it.

The study was constructed round a series of case studies of mainstream English medium schools. The researchers made visits to the four different schools to observe each school in action and carry out semi-structured interviews with teachers in the school, as well as with the principal of the school, and where possible with students and parents, too. Some of these interviews were conducted online and some, especially with students, took the form of group interviews. Where necessary the interviews were transcribed and prepared for analysis by student assistants to the researchers in Lebanon. The actual analysis was carried out by the researchers using a standard thematic approach to analysing quali-tative data. Some of this analysis was carried out in Lebanon and some in the UK, the researchers keeping in touch with each other by email. Although the research was intended to be carried out in English, participants were allowed to respond in French or in Arabic (the local national language) with which one or more of the researchers was familiar.

At the first school the researchers visited, teacher respondents began answering online interviews in English – the language in which they taught – but then reverted to French (the language which they spoke at school) or to Arabic. In other schools teachers took a similar approach, shifting the process of the research project to meet their needs as well as those of the researchers.

---

Writing rather than speaking in a second language may help to empower some non-native speakers (Mann and Stewart, 2000). The anonymity of online research denies people the potential embarrassment (loss of social status/'face', loss of power) of trying to express themselves orally in ways they consider less than sufficiently fluent. In a study that involved East Asian participants, online communication enabled more direct communication and greater self-disclosure (Ma, 1996). Participants had less fear of rejection or disagreement in the virtual environment. Being unable to discriminate subtly the social situation and the anticipated perspectives of the researcher may help participants to develop highly personal and intimate conversa-tions (James, 2003).

# Negotiating Participation in Online Research Projects

The inequalities of power in research projects arise from the positioning of participants within it. Like 'hosts' (Derrida, 2000), researchers police the boundaries of their (online) research projects. They safeguard what they perceive as its core values, purposes and process. However the nature of their power is essentially disciplinary (Cavanagh, 2007; Foucault, 1977). It provides a means of social control by monitoring people's practices in a faceless arena, to make sure they conform to the norms developed in that online research community (see Box 7.3).

The social relationships that researchers construct with the participants of their projects represent asymmetric power relationships. This suggests that all social relationships are 'bearers of power' (Massey, 1994, in Rodgers, 2004: 281). So space/time relationships between people, for example researchers and research participants, particularly in online research, have to be concerned with how time and space help to construct those power relationships. Synchronous and asynchronous online interviewing can create spaces in which participants can explore their changing self-perceptions. Synchronous communications, however, whether in chat rooms or on VLEs, impose restrictive time frames on participants, especially when they live in different time zones. Asynchronous communications, on the other hand, seem to offer participants and researchers considerable flexibility in their use of time.

As indicated in Chapter 2, to gain entry to research sites, researchers may need to mediate with the moderator or elder of a discussion forum or community (Kim, 2000, in Bishop, 2006). In such sites, these elders are likely to be the people who post frequently to a particular online forum and try to assert norms for engagement with that community. They play a role similar to those of the 'old timers' trying to sustain the norms of practice within their communities by inducting newer members into them (Lave and Wenger, 1991). Moderators and administrators of online fora/communities also act as powerful gatekeepers to their communities. This is because they often have technical expertise, 'technopower' (Jordan, 1999), which they can use to control the processes of data gathering by researchers and connections between participants and researchers.

In online research projects, participants can have a sense of marginality as they never see the researchers and are only in contact with them intermittently. They can feel deprived of a sense of engagement in a human conversation and, so, of a sense of power to present their own voice. Such a sense of marginality can lead to a lack of sense of commitment to a research project. It can lead to participants who perceive themselves in this way taking limited part or dropping out altogether. The construction of democratic processes in research projects may help to counter this (Oakley, 1981), by helping participants to perceive themselves as influential core members of a project community, able to influence its development and to gain benefits both from participation in it and from the outcomes of it (Wenger, 1998).

Collaborative approaches to online research shift the nature of engagement that participants feel with their research projects, helping them to have a greater sense of being core members of them (Bakardjieva and Feenberg, 2000; LeBesco, 2004). This can help participants meet their interests, that is, it enhances their power and self-identity as a valued person in the project. Such shifts in power from researchers to participants can be viewed as a form of distributing power and leadership from the originators of a project to its newer members (Gronn, 2000). One of the ways in which participants can be empowered is by allowing their discussion topics to become contained within the original research agenda of the project. Researchers need to handle this sensitively to ensure that they attain their original research objectives, but enrich these with those other topics of discussion that the participants perceive as important. Another way is to allow participants as much control over the timing of their responses as possible within the constraints of the formal structures of a research project.

In our studies, we hoped that by allowing power to be redistributed to participants within the research projects, and by investing in a more collaborative relationship with the participants, more democratic and enriched narrative exchanges would take place (Busher, 2001; James, 2003). This is illustrated in Box 7.3. Collaborative relationships involve mutuality and reciprocity (Oakley, 1981). This was reflected in our studies, by our participants' lack of inhibition and frankness in their discussions as they wrote about how their identities were socially constructed and multi-faceted.

---

### Box 7.3    Shifting power relationships in online research projects

At the start of our interviews we believed we were in more powerful positions epistemologically than were our participants. This was because we shaped the agenda of the discussions and had access to the relevant literatures underpinning the conceptual frameworks of the studies (Easterby-Smith et al., 1991). We were also in more powerful positions bureaucratically. We created the organisational structures of the studies by providing the key research questions and methods of research as well as the 'rules of engagement' between participants and the research project.

The online discussions of our research projects were sites of struggle. Our research conversations with participants were engagements through which participants sought to construct and convey meanings and stories about their identities and practices in particular contexts. In doing so, they not only wrestled with the questions we posed to them but struggled with the contexts in which they worked at being and becoming practitioners in particular fields. In addition the participants, as well as ourselves, had to wrestle with the unfamiliar processes of conducting online qualitative research interviews.

---

However, as our participants began to understand the properties of space/time asynchronously they began to use these to enrich their discussions and fit their responses to the rhythms of the busy press of their lives. It gave them the space/ opportunity to develop their thoughts more deeply than they might have done in a real-time face-to-face interview where the rhythm of the interaction might have been more strongly controlled by a researcher and by contextual factors, such as the other demands on participants' time.

Participants began to assert control of time and speed of response despite our attempts to set and keep to a pre-ordained time frame for the research project. So email interviews that had been scheduled to take a matter of two to three weeks eventually extended in many cases over several months. Through time it became apparent that the participants exercised influence, too, in the shaping of the research project community, and changed the nature of the research process. Prompt replies, we discovered, were not actually necessary, particularly when slower ones gave opportunity for more powerful reflection on the main focus of the studies.

Within the social, intellectual and chronological spaces that existed in our studies, our participants began to respond to our questions and prompts at a time schedule that suited their own professional and personal lives, rather than that initially set by the researchers. This marked the beginnings of a transfer of some ownership of the research projects to our participants through the process of narrative construction. Participants who began by apologising for being late in responding to us ended up, like ourselves, taking it for granted that replies would happen on an irregular basis to fit in with their lives. However a subtext of this, after some members of each research project had dropped out, was that the responses would be sent, even if only in due course. As the research projects progressed, researchers and participants alike came to accept these 'delays' in the email interviews as the new norms of practice. These reflected shifts in the balance of power within the research projects.

An important element in creating collaborative approaches to research is the construction of trust between members. Interpersonal knowledge and the negotiation and emergence of a culture in a community are interrelated with flows of power in and through that community, as the foregoing shows.

One source of power always open to participants in research projects is the choice of how much personal and/or private information to disclose in the public or semi-public fora of online group interviews and communities. This complexity of self, identity and perspective occurs in face-to-face research as well as in online research. It is particularly evident in online interviewing, where it is not always possible for researchers to verify the identity of the participants with whom they are speaking without prior knowledge of them.

Against participants' power to withhold information, even if they choose to join a research project, are the efforts of researchers to construct a welcoming and supportive environment for research. The faceless nature of the online interview challenges researchers to find new means of constructing the informal and socially oriented verbal and non-verbal signals that they often use to create and sustain such an environment. Although these predominantly occur in the prelude or postlude to an interview, or to a whole research project, they can also occur throughout its course.

One way researchers may try to build a supportive environment is in terms of conversations being constructed in an informal dialogue and developing a sense of intimacy between participants (Carter, 2005: 155–6). However, this reflects Western values of informal relationships between more and less powerful participants in a community (Hofstede, 1991), for example researchers and other participants in a project. So it may be of less use in non-Western or multinational contexts, where some participants may expect dialogues to take more formal styles of engagement between participants. Another means of trying to suggest friendliness is through the use of emoticons to begin to indicate feelings in the text/speech acts of online research. However, for some participants these attempts at informality may be socially uncomfortable, especially if they come from cultures where low formality between people of different status (researcher and participant, for example) is uncommon if not unacceptable.

Restating the framework of an online research interview is another means through which researchers can (re)assert their authority in a research project. In doing this they might remind participants of what they have agreed to, or of the preferred norms of interpersonal exchange for the research project. Such actions help to confirm (or deny) to a participant why he/she has consented to take part in that project, that is, agreed to a social contract with the researcher(s) when joining the project. Providing relevant information to participants about the project at certain points in it helps researchers to sustain the contract entered in to by researchers and participants. Failure to provide this may lead to participants withholding, even if only temporarily, their consent to continue to participate, that is, exert their power to withdraw from the contract. Researchers need to establish their credibility to overcome this problem (Sanders, 2005).

Participants can assert their power by taking the research conversations in directions of their own choice as they seek to make sense of the experiences being investigated by the researchers. However, this assertion of participants' control raises the potential risk of research interviews having an increasingly selective focus. It might even risk important points in the original research project specification not being fully discussed or poorly developed. In contrast, project interview schedules act as aide-memoires to remind researchers and other participants of the original foci of the research and can be used to avoid such narrowing of them. Researchers can refer to these to re-assert the original research agenda to members of the research project community. But in doing so they re-assert their power and diminish the (possibly illusory) collaborative culture they may have tried to establish in the research project to sustain participants' membership of it. In Chapter 8 there is more extensive discussion of the importance of collaborative cultures to sustaining (online qualitative) research projects.

## Conclusion

As we have discussed, the Internet is altering people's senses of identity by giving them new opportunities for communicating with people and gaining (control over) information. In engaging with the new systems of communication and understanding how to manipulate its rules, people are able to assert their agency to reconstruct their identities in new ways (Giddens, 1991, 1984). However, online communications also deprive participants and researchers of some senses of control in the construction of discussions, and deprive some potential participants absolutely if they do not have access to adequate (or any) Internet connections. For the former this can challenge individuals to work more intensively on projects of themselves (Giddens, 1991) as well on formal work projects, such as the construction of knowledge through research.

Researchers and participants in online research projects have to struggle to (re)assert themselves in the context of this still relatively new medium through engaging with it and its associated rule systems. The nature of online communications makes it more difficult to develop some of the assumptions of shared views and perspectives that may develop in face-to-face qualitative research projects that have a common purpose, and facilitate the interactions of researchers and participants. So although the Internet provides researchers with the potential to cross geographical, cultural and linguistic boundaries, researchers must be aware of not only with whom they communicate online, but the impact this has on those who participate in their research projects. Such tensions in power relations do not go away in the anonymity of the Internet. It highlights how the inequalities of power need to be ethically addressed in order to facilitate maximum participant engagement in online research projects, as we discussed in Chapter 5.

The reality is that while online qualitative research interviews can increase the scope and range of social science research, the digital divide also means that it can be very geographically specific, limiting who we 'speak' to and whose lives we engage with, especially in certain societies/cultures. Of course, this can be greatly facilitated if researchers are able to have at least some face-to-face contact with other participants in the research. If physical interpersonal contact or presence is not possible technical solutions such as webcams, blogs and secure websites may offer important opportunities for social networking as adjuncts to online qualitative research. In the 21st century, the Internet does not have to simply reply on text-only communication (see, for example, Hookway, 2008; Phippen, 2007).

However, the use of online research can enable more direct communication and greater self-disclosure in certain cultural contexts (as our research has demonstrated) if research participants can find ways of re-asserting themselves, and establish an online presence by giving voice to their own values and personal and social needs. In doing so they can re-negotiate the parameters of engagement in the online research project, of which they have membership. This leads to the small/micro-cultures of such projects shifting to become more collaborative, although researchers still appear to have access to considerable influence and power to shape their processes.

## Practical Tips for Online Researchers

- Remember the international frameworks of Internet communications.
- Make your communication sites as secure as possible.
- Develop collaborative approaches for online qualitative research.
- Help participants have a sense of being core members of your research project.
- Recognise that participants want gains out of a project, e.g. the project benefits people; they gain new knowledge; they have self-identity as a valued person in the project.
- Allow participants' discussion agenda items to become contained within the original research agenda of the project.
- Allow participants as much control over the timing of their responses as possible within the constraints of the formal structures of a research project.
- Be aware of participants' language abilities and help participants makes sense of their exchanges with you.

### Further Reading

Evans, K.F. (2004) *Maintaining Community in the Information Age: The Importance of Trust, Place and Situated Knowledge*. Melbourne: Palgrave Macmillan.
Foucault, M. (1976) 'Truth and power', in C. Gordon (ed.), (1980) *Power/Knowledge: Selected Interviews and Other Writings by Michel Foucault, 1972–1977*. New York: Pantheon Books. pp. 78–108.
Giddens, A. (1984) *The Constitution of Society*. Berkley, CA: University of California.

# EIGHT

## Investigating and Deconstructing the Cultures of Online Research Communities

> Overview: this chapter focuses on the interrogation of meanings in the third spaces of online qualitative research projects. It begins by considering how such spaces lead to the negotiation of cultural hybridity and the construction of small cultures by researchers and participants engaged individually or as groups in the text/speech acts of online exchanges. In turn, this leads, first, to consideration of the nature of the cultures of online research communities. Second, it leads to a discussion of the analysis of online discourses that are constructed in these disembodied third spaces.

### Introduction

The Internet provides a social space in which people can construct participation in different types of social groups. These groups construct sub-cultures (Williams, 2006) or small cultures (Holliday, 2004). They reflect the socially constructed beliefs and values of the members of communities. The culture of each community is based on members' lived experiences in various communities whether corporeal or virtual, and their cultural and social capital (Bourdieu, 1986). It is therefore important to understand the contexts in which people live and work in order to make sense of the discourses they construct. Group cultures often form around some particular interest or purpose, such as a research project.

Small cultures are constructed by groups and individuals for many reasons. One is as a means of coming to terms with each other to create a common or agreed framework for practices to achieve common purposes. These cultures emerge in the interstices of the formal or informal processes of an institution or across institutions or social networks, and are considered as third spaces (Bhabha, 1994). Research projects are an example of groups that are formed in the interstices of people's other social and institutional interactions. In these, researchers and participants negotiate the construction of small cultures for their research projects. In and through the third spaces of research conversations people from different cultural backgrounds create a hybrid culture that is neither entirely theirs nor entirely that of the others in the developing community. Such cultures only exist for the duration of its members' engagement in that research community because it is a social construct of theirs.

In these third spaces, members of a research community 'elaborate strategies of selfhood – singular or communal – that initiate new signs of identity, and innovative sites of collaboration and contestation, in the act of defining the idea of society itself' (Bhabha, 1994: 2). As noted in the previous chapter, participants engaging in such discourses may come from very different national and local cultures. People's social relationships are tied to the social frameworks from which they come, for example 'kinship ties, social duty or traditional obligation' (Giddens, 1991: 6). People engage in emotional and psychological work to transform these so they can build trust with other people and create communities. In such circumstances, each participant's perceptions of research, as well as of appropriate interpersonal communications, may be constructed around very different norms and concerns.

In the disembodied arena of online qualitative research these different perspectives can make it difficult for researchers and participants to know how to analyse and interpret (make sense of) the conversations they have with each other. As language is the main way in which individuals communicate with each other in their online exchanges, language can sometimes be used creatively to convey individuals' lived realities of their world, their perspectives and the contexts in which they live. So analysing the data that emerges through online research conversations is both problematic and fascinating.

This chapter considers how researchers and participants negotiate the construction of small cultures for their research projects. It then debates the nature of online communication that is at the heart of the construction of cultures, before moving on to discuss how data from online research projects can be captured and analysed, particularly through the use of group interviews, in these disembodied third spaces.


## Constructing Cultures in the Third Spaces of Online Communities

There are many types of online community spaces serving various functions and meeting the needs of their members in a variety of ways. Researchers may also seek out spaces which provide potential participants for a research project. These communities can provide more naturalistic settings for gathering data. Such communities can allow researchers to gain additional insights from the discourse and interaction taking place between participants either synchronously or asynchronously.

Each space (community) has its own culture and rules of conduct that define how people should interact with each other within it and what the purposes and process of it are. The cultural narratives of a community help to build its cohesion and identity, in part through defining how it differs from others (Williams, 2006). They offer a framework of norms enshrined in rules, language, ceremonies and rituals that help members of a community to try to sustain its existing identity and address problems they face (Trompenaars and Woolliams, 2003). They mark the boundaries of particular social and institutional entities and drive shared patterns of behaviour (Robbins, 2003). So cultures become important means by which societies and communities reproduce themselves (Bourdieu, 1990; Bourdieu and Passeron, 1977). Culture provides a means through which members of a community create and sustain meanings of their community (Levinson et al., 1996). However, this process is always in flux as situations change, creating a conduit and site of power (Doherty, 2007). A community's culture is likely to change over time because of its members' interactions with their socio-political contexts as well as with each other.

Unsurprisingly, some members are more powerful in shaping this construction than others, as argued in Chapter 7. For researchers this is problematic. What may appear as the authentic social identity of a community may only reflect the dominant discourse of that community. This may be sustained by only a relatively few influential members (Williams, 2006). Further, the description of a community by people who are outside it may also be in conflict with the views of its members. Evans (2004) found that a group of women in northern England who lacked access to the Internet were misrepresented as being uninterested in gaining access to it. So researchers investigating online communities need to collect the voices of peripheral and core participants (Wenger, 1998), old hands and novices (Lave and Wenger, 1991), gatekeepers/hosts (Derrida, 2000) and external perspectives, if they are to gain an authentic understanding and membership of that community. So, online communities can be considered as communities of practice (Lave and Wenger, 1991). They link participants' practice or work in a research project to wider constellations of academic norms and practices (Wenger, 1998). Through negotiation with other members over time, participants come to (re)define some aspects of their identities in relation to the shared practices of a particular community, for example, a research project.

The (small) cultures (Holliday, 2004) that emerge in online communities are not those of a 'radically new frontier' (Doherty, 2007: 1) but similar in process to those constructed by face-to-face communities. In any community, people's 'cultural identities need to be understood as positions forged and displayed in the contingencies of interactions with others' (Doherty, 2007: 6). The values that guide people's daily activities are derived from their communities' cultures which, in turn, are shaped by the histories of people individually and collectively and of their communities. These values help a community's members interpret events and decide what decisions to take in their interactions with other people.

The identities people construct from and through the cultural milieu that they inhabit, as well as the cultural and social capital they gain (Bourdieu, 1986), cannot reasonably be taken as givens that they carry with them from birth. 'Conventional assumptions of culture as coherent and coterminous with social background, language use, regions, religion, or ethnicity have become impossible to sustain' (Eisenhart, 2001, in Doherty, 2007: 6). So people's constructed identities tend to shift through time. In turn, the cultures of the communities of which they have membership reflect this. However, the cultures of communities also reflect the dominant macro-culture of the society in which they are embedded. The macro-cultural contexts include factors such as national and local discourses around gender, ethnicity, the economy and the socio-economic status of its members.

In the globalised spaces of online communities these cultural contexts become problematic (Doherty, 2007). What counts as national or local to one person is likely to be distant to or not understood by another participant. So in online groups this enhances the possibility of people misunderstanding each other. Each person in an international online group brings her/his cultural heritage to the interpersonal interactions within it. Such 'borderline engagements of cultural difference may as often be consensual as conflictual' (Bhabha, 1994: 3). For example, people from different macro-cultures may not share the same view of what constitutes normal interpersonal relationships in research and this may generate tension between participants and researchers across boundaries of space and time.

Online communities are likely to change through time through the interactions of their members with each other and with the socio-political contexts in which they are embedded. Small cultures help their members to engage successfully with the dominant discourses of social and organisational culture which surround them. It allows them to retain some of their own preferred values and beliefs while acknowledging the influence on their communities, of values and policies held in their institutional and societal contexts. These external values and policies are mediated to these small communities by powerful peripheral members (Wenger, 1998), some of whom are hierarchically distant from the other members of a community.

Full membership of a community does not occur immediately for an individual when they join it, or without conflict. In part, membership is developed through people's induction to a community as they learn the accepted norms of behaviour and practice. Membership is slowly constructed through people gradually choosing to engage and disclose themselves more fully (Joinson, 2005; Lee, 2006). In online research projects, as participants' negotiations and conversations lead to greater intimacy and self-disclosure, participants also develop senses of tension between what they wish to disclose and to whom (Carter, 2005; Williams, 2006), that is, they question how far they want to be committed to the relationship. This tension reflects the power differentials between the members of a developing online community, reflecting who is authorised or appears to be authorised to act in certain ways.

The attenuated time and space of communication on the Internet is an important element in the construction of the hybrid cultures of online communities. It creates a different rhythm to that of face-to-face conversations, in part because people can only perform their interactions through the text/speech acts of online communications. This, in turn, alters the quality of interaction between researchers and other participants.

The processes of symbolic interaction between members of communities is one of an on-going negotiation of identities that never reaches closure. Bhabha (1994) uses the metaphor of the stairwell to indicate the connective nature of on-going dialogues in time and space. 'The hither and thither of the stairwell, temporal movement and the passage that it allows, prevents identities at either end of it from settling into primordial polarities' (Bhabha, 1994: 5). This 'opens up the possibility of cultural hybridity that entertains difference without an assumed or imposed hierarchy' (Bhabha, 1994: 5). So our present selves, which perhaps we only partially understand, are complex and dynamic and in dynamic dialogue with our past selves. Both of these are enacted in a variety of social circumstances and cultural milieu.

It is this process of reflection on past and present self that online research can investigate through the use of unstructured interviews. The latter encourage participants to construct narratives in to which they weave their present and past perspectives of their experiences of being in particular contexts. These new constructions of identity interact with and inform people's performances of themselves in other online or offline communities and social interactions.

> To dwell 'in the beyond' is ... to be part of a revisionary time, a return to the present to
> redescribe our cultural contemporaneity; to re-inscribe our human historic commonality ...
> In that sense, then, the intervening space 'beyond' becomes a space of intervention in the
> here and now. (Bhabha, 1994: 10)

These constructions of identities by online participants are often presented to others as well as to themselves as narratives. Such narratives are means of social identification (Williams, 2006: 177). Through them people portray who they think they are in the particular social networks and communities with which they are connected peripherally or centrally. These narratives change with the different situations and communities in which people find themselves (Zhao, 2006). However, this also occurs in face-to-face relationships (Whitty, 2002). When online representations of self are authentic they often keep reasonably close to people's embodied and lived selves (Williams, 2006), as argued in Chapter 6. It makes it easier for people to present consistent and coherent selves. It also helps other participants in (online) conversations to feel more confident of the authenticity of the conversations in which they are engaging (Carter, 2005).

The conversations in which people engage online can lead to the creation of a small culture (Holliday, 2004) especially if the conversations are for a specific purpose. This is the process by which online research projects are constructed. Box 8.1 shows that small cultures have three main spheres of action (Holliday, 1994).

## Box 8.1 Constructing a small culture in an online research project

The three spheres of action for constructing small cultures can be illustrated through our own research projects:

*Psycho-cultural features:* These include elements such as tacit protocols governing classroom interaction and relationships between staff (or researchers) and between staff and students (or other participants). As our online research projects developed, collaborative discourses emerged between ourselves and our participants. These reflected the developing shared meanings of the members of each research project.

*The micro-political process:* These are illustrated by the way in which participants came increasingly to negotiate the pace and manner in which they responded to researchers' questions, as well as shaped the agenda of the conversations.

*The rubrics:* These help to maintain order informally, perhaps through constructing administrative frameworks to help a community function. In the case of our research projects these rubrics (shown in Chapter 4) provided the frameworks which guided the interactions of our research project communities (they were originally established by the researchers). It was these that were contested by participants as the micro-cultures of the projects developed and the original dominant discourses, created by the researchers, were modified.

### Colonising Spaces: Constructing Online Research Communities

Online research is a form of intellectual work through which knowledge is constructed and tested (Hodkinson, 2004). This work involves the interactions of participants with each other and with researchers for a purpose: to create successful research projects. To achieve this, researchers and participants have to engage in a variety of practices. Research projects that involve online group interviews take on many of the characteristics of communities. They are often built initially around asymmetrical power relationships and within recognised contextual frameworks for carrying out such work. The researchers who set them up act as moderators (gatekeepers) inducting new members (participants) into increasing degrees of belonging to the unique social-cultural practices of each project. However if a researcher is trying to join an online community, such as a discussion forum or chat room to carry out research, he/she is likely to be perceived as a 'novice' in the community so will need to be inducted into its practices by the elders. This will help a researcher better understand the social context that is being researched. In time, this may lead some participants to move from initial peripheral participation to core membership creating more frank exchanges between participants. In such research projects participants and researchers can construct shared meanings, norms and values, but these too can be contested by participants, leading to group flaming and intense frustration of members.

The relationships between group members can create small cultures (Holliday, 2004). They use symbolic markers to reify boundaries between themselves and other people (Williams, 2006: 189). Members draw on elements from different dominant and marginalised cultural discourses to construct a new emergent set of cultural norms for the (emergent) community. 'The flows and technologies associated with globalisation have blurred previously clear boundaries that spatially mapped cultures' (Doherty, 2007: 7). So, members of online communities in the study of Williams (2006) often talked about their cultural spaces in essentialist terms. It helped to make their community real.

For many members, online communities become the primary source of participation. In them, participants construct new voices to engage successfully with a group of people with whom they may not share social and cultural norms. Engaging with and in the hybrid cultures of online research projects is a transformative process for all concerned. 'It is the space of intervention emerging in the cultural interstices that introduces creative invention into existence ... There is a return to the performance of identity as iteration, the re-creation of the self' (Bhabha, 1994: 12).

In online research projects, creativity occurs because participants are often encouraged to go beyond the boundaries of their present in various ways. In some cases it is to explore their understandings of their past: as students, as learners, as novice professionals. In others it is to explore their views on future social constructions or processes: staff development, decision making, teaching certain groups of students. Sometimes it is to reflect on their present practice in ways that challenge their taken-for-granted notions of self and cultural identity, and the power relations associated with those. So:

> the present [is] ... no longer simply envisaged as a break or bonding with the past and the future, no longer a synchronic presence. Our proximate self-presence, our public image, comes to be revealed for its discontinuities, its inequalities, its minorities. (Bhabha, 1994: 6)

For communities to work, members have to perceive collectively and individually the worth of and symbolic value of continuing to participate in them (Williams, 2006: 174). In many cases this perception is related to the supposed economic or social worth of the community. However, the benefits are less clear for those participating in an online community as part of a research project. People joining them do not seem to get any material gain from them, although they may have altruistic reasons for agreeing to take part. Further, the intrusiveness of collecting interview data from such communities has the added potential of causing harm and jeopardising the safety of personal disclosure. It can also destroy the supporting function of the online community (Bowker and Tuffin, 2004: 232). In such circumstances, the quality of interpersonal relationships that researchers can build with their participants is crucial for keeping a research project afloat.

Building commitment to a research project has several elements. One is the construction of shared purpose, perhaps to achieve perceived benefits whether shared or not, or experienced personally or altruistically. Teachers may choose to be involved in a research project because they think it will benefit students' learning, for example, whether or not they personally gain anything from taking part in that project. Another is, initially at least, that potential participants are likely to expect researchers to behave like researchers (Matthews, 2006). This is inscribed in the developing community of a new research project through the actions and expectations of the hosts of the project: the researchers. This involves researchers explaining clearly the social and communications structures for participating in conversations about the topic that is the focus of the project. Where researchers have to publicly notify an online community about their project, such practice helps to establish their credibility amongst other participants and allow the latter to begin to trust the former, rather than endanger participants' privacy and safety.

Constructing trust between researchers and participants is crucial in qualitative research whether online or face-to-face. Trust is closely related to a sense of ownership of a research project. This is strongly linked to the extent to which participants have confidence in the research environment which researchers construct. A major source of confidence for participants is when researchers explain how they intend to carry out a study following recognised ethical practices, of the sort discussed in Chapter 5. These indicate what actions researchers must take to keep participants from harm.

Participants' willingness to join research projects reflects the degree of trust that the participants have in the researchers. As one participant in one of our studies said:

> Clearly it helped me to know who was on the other end of the line. I'm not sure what 'persuasion' one can use if one were to try this approach 'cold'. (Busher, 2001)

The second sentence suggests that participants unfamiliar with online communication may be unwilling to join online research projects, especially those focused on more personally revelatory qualitative online research. On the other hand, participants familiar with online communication are likely to develop their trust of other participants in ways similar to those by people in face-to-face communication (Whitty, 2002). As people get to know each other through their text/speech acts online so they develop a view of the other that allows them to develop trust in them to a greater or lesser degree.

Trust affects the extent to which participants are willing to be open and honest with researchers. It sustains the process of exchange between participants and researchers in the continuing life of a research project. However, its construction and maintenance is a cultural artefact to which participants and researcher(s) contribute for their mutual benefit. As one of the participants in our studies commented:

> It is very important the interviewer/interviewee relationship is existing and positive. Establishing a good rapport and background generally is as in every interview essential – especially in case of sensitive questions ... (Busher, 2001)

One particular manifestation of trust, particularly in online communities, is the development of friendship. It is an important quality in the construction of online relationships, particularly where participants are sharing the same social space (Carter, 2005). Friendship often begins with meetings in public space online which give participants an opportunity to test out each other's identities. Although this happens in ways similar to the processes of developing face-to-face relationships (Lee, 2006; Whitty, 2002), online the absence of non-verbal and visual clues means individuals can be more open about who they are. However, this requires researchers to be more proactive in initiating, negotiating and progressing online relationships. Similarly, where people join an online research project with little if any previous knowledge of the researchers, mutually exploring each other's identities as part of the initiation into the project can be beneficial in the early phases of conversations or interviews.

## The Hybridity of Communicative Space in Online Research

Central to the construction of communities is how people communicate with each other (Barton and Tusting, 2005). In online exchanges this is largely through text/speech acts without the support of the visual and non-verbal clues that occur in face-to-face communication.

The Internet is a virtual social arena that encompasses co-temporal relationships and co-spatial relationships as well as relationships between people in different times and places. It allows interpersonal communication to take place either asynchronously or synchronously, in ways that may not be possible in the face-to-face world. These communications can be constructed through multi-user groups and/or one-to-one relationships. These allow participants and researchers to understand personal and shared meanings when it is not possible to meet face-to-face because of constraints of time and space (Murray and Sixsmith, 1998).

Communication in online research include a construction of participants' relationships with social situations and with the researcher (Mann and Stewart, 2000). They also provide an extensive language for interpreting multi-layered social experiences (Bowker and Tuffin, 2004). However, online communication occurs without the 'markers of context based in physical appearance, time, place or position' (Kibby, 2005: 772).

Online communication is a 'communicative space' (Crystal, 2001) in which text combines a 'spoken' style of writing that can be deliberative, stilted, in/formal and include extended utterances. When participants are concentrating on the content of their messages, the nature of the communication may be 'fairly close to being characteristic of the writer's habits' and preferences in oral discourse' (Davis and Brewer, 1997: 24). So the writing will have conversational qualities. It is a text/speech act, a hybrid that none-the-less has its own coherence. The text that emerges in online communications is both text and speech, document and interaction (Hine, 2000). Internet users directly type their thoughts into the keyboard and immediately send messages, as though they are engaged in conversation (Barnes, 2004).

Such hybridity has also been defined as 'electronic discourse' (Davis and Brewer, 1997: 2) – writing that often reads as though it has been spoken ('writing talking'). Consequently the written text is 'laden with conversation like conventions' (Davis and Brewer, 1997: 156). Language is used as if individuals were engaged in conversation. This description reinforces how conventions of oral and written discourse can be adapted by individuals to suit their own interactive strategies and styles of communication (Denzin, 1999).

The dual nature of the communication has been characterised by Mann and Stewart (2000: 182) as a 'linguistic pantheon', that takes two key forms: conversation and writing.

### Conversation

In many ways synchronous and asynchronous communication online is close to talk. Individuals type quickly, phonetically and expressively to capture elements of their online lives. This informality is illustrated in Box 8.2. It leads to a relaxing of established conventions of social contact, especially in the absence of reduced situational context cues (Kibby, 2005). This dynamic dimension to conversational turn-taking can either take seconds (in synchronous chat) or days (asynchronously). Such informality helps to construct an exchange of correspondence that approximates to a conversation. Email communication can be construed as a form of 'secondary orality' (Kibby, 2005: 771) because it is based on writing, but privileges orality as the dynamics of an exchange. So it reflects a participatory event. As consistency of meaning, albeit with increasing complexity, emerges through these exchanges, participants gain a sense that they are developing shared understandings.

---

### Box 8.2    Online communication as a hybrid form

Online communication is a hybrid of both spoken and written language. The linguistic features can vary enormously depending on text-type and the personal characteristics of the individual sending the text (including age, identity, gender). They include the use of:

(i)     informal phonetic spelling (are you gonna do wot I did)

(ii)    absence of capitalisation (got yer email – i'll be over later)

(iii)   use of interjections (at last – phew!)

(iv)   flaming, aggressive tones in online communication (I'm really ANGR-RRRRY!!!!!!!!!!!!!!!!!!!)

(v)    in-terms and abbreviations  (BTW have you heard about the meeting?) and telegraphic language  (Have you forwarded the email? Will do, but am not back in office until Tuesday)

(vi)   use of interaction features (I'll be over later in the day, ok?)

(vii)  streams of conscious writing (just one more thing, do I want to go on another shopping trip? do I?, oh well I have to decide that when I need to!)

(viii) paralinguistics and graphics such as multiple letters (Helloooooo!)

(ix)   capitalisation (shouting), little or excessive punctuation

(x)    emoticons (looking forward to meeting soon ☺ :-) )

---

To some extent, the examples in Box 8.2 can be likened to the linguistic qualities of note-taking in which thoughts and expressions are abbreviated, and include typing errors to save time and effort (Mann and Stewart, 2000). They are also reminiscent of 'flitting language' (Stewart and Williams, 2005: 399) that can create the perception of a face-to-face conversation through 'chat'.

### Writing

The time and space embedded in asynchronous email allows participants in online communications to reflect on their responses and reply at a time convenient to them. Thinking about what to write before despatching it, locates participants' email communication with traditional forms of writing. It is not intentional speech, even though it is often read as if it were

(Denzin, 1999). Yet, unlike conversation, before online communication is sent it is spell-checked, edited, rearranged and sometimes inflected with emoticons. So once written, the conversation (speech) is destroyed (Denzin, 1999). The examples of online writing in Box 8.2 reinforce how online communication has the features of traditional written communication as well as some characteristics of spoken communication (Duncan-Howell, 2007).

## Social and Linguistic Clues in Online Research Communications

Normal social frameworks of face-to-face encounters between researchers and participants are those in which both interpret the social characteristics of the other, either verbally or non-verbally through gesture, tone of voice and facial expressions. The absence of these in online communication can represent a diminution in the quality of the data gathering compared to the richness of face-to-face communications (Bowker and Tuffin, 2004). However, 'we may underestimate the presence of the body in electronic communication, and over estimate the power of the body to facilitate the face-to-face situation' (Seymour, 2001: 162). The absence of social presence and reduced visual cues can actually make participants feel more comfortable about personal disclosure online, and encourage them to open up in 'a way that would not happen with the spoken word' (James, 2007: 971). This is because they feel less inhibited by the researcher's physical presence, affording participants greater freedom to express themselves without fear of judgment (Bowker and Tuffin, 2004).

Online communication removes many paralinguistic modes of information, such as intonation, gestures and facial expression (Bowker and Tuffin, 2004). Some progress has been made in developing means of representing these in text (see Box 8.2). For example, socio-emotional aspects of body language, nodding and eye contact, as well as of voice inflections can be conveyed by emoticons and abbreviations. Or exaggerated punctuation and capitalisation can be used to emphasise tone and strength of feeling on a particular topic:

> I WASN'T ALWAYS SURE THAT I KNEW WHAT YOU WERE GEETING AT ... SOME OF THE QUESTIONS SEEMED TO OVERLAP AND I WAS CONCERNED ABOUT MAYBE WE WERE SOMETIMES COMING AT SOMETHING FROM DIFFERENT DIRECTIONS AND MAYBE IN E-MAIL COMMUNICATIONS CLARIFICATION IS NOT ALWAYS EASY:)!
> (James, 2003: 92)

An example of the use of emoticons and other textual features to convey meaning can be seen in the study by Markham (2004b). Scattered through the text of her participants were utterances such as 'LOL,!!<:-)' as well as other interjections. She interpreted this as her correspondent sending multiple messages from the moment her interaction with the participant began. Typical interactions with her participants included:

**LOL** This is way cool! I have never been asked for an interview before:)

I am interested in talking to: Could you be more spesific about what questions you will ask? Just to let me know when you want to talk, and I will try to accomidate!:)

My cyberfriends and I liked to roleplay … we went on fantastic adventures over the net. The only limit was our imagineations. Not anything like in the real world!! I am shy by nature … I am also a big fan of Shahspear langue. I can use that style of speaking, and not be shy about on the net:) (Markham, 2004b: 148)

The participant's 'electronic discourse' had manipulated language using typographical and spelling errors in order to express herself. However, as many of the examples in this chapter highlight, such texts can be littered with grammatical errors, spelling mistakes and netlingo such as abbreviations and acronyms (Thurlow et al., 2004). The meanings or intentionality of these may not be clear to a researcher without further interrogation of the views of participants. It illustrates how synchronous and asynchronous online interactions are constructed as a hybrid of speech and writing.

Online communication uses a frame of conventional vocabularies of meaning (Seymour, 2001). These vocabularies are mediated by people to try to convey meanings that, in face-to-face communication, might be conveyed by non-verbal cues. Consequently the surface features of online text often carry additional meanings to the ones with which they are nominally invested in written communications. For example, if a participant types in capitals or uses alternative spellings, what 'meaningful' information on the participant's identity and culture can a reader glean? It implies that it would be inappropriate for a researcher to correct such typing when presenting it as evidence in a report, since that might ignore and misrepresent a participant's deliberate presentation of self (Markham, 2004b: 150). Qualitative online researchers need to be aware of this issue and reflect on their own communication styles in the research process (Kivits, 2005).

## Collecting and Analysing Data in and from Naturalistic and Constructed Online Settings

In online communities, the challenge is to capture the contingent cultural productions and understandings in the ephemeral settings that people inhabit. There are a variety of means by which researchers can capture such data. In her study, Doherty (2007) thought email interviews were a good enough means of accessing participants' discourses of their experiences of online learning. However, individual interviews can be carried out in chat rooms equally as well as with email. The former is likely to be a synchronous interview while the latter might be either synchronous or asynchronous. The group perspectives of members of online communities can be captured using focus groups or group discussions/interviews. Both these forms can be constructed online through using discussion boards in VLEs or web-boards. There are also non-intrusive methods of data collection online such as document-based research (Walker, 2000), as well as ethnographic studies (Reed, 2004; Williams, 2006) of online communities undertaken through forms of participant observation.

The discussion here focuses particularly on the use and analysis of interviews in online research. In all types of interviews participants enter with some awareness of their role as a social actor. As such they have privileged access to personal experiences which they choose to share with others (Davis et al., 2004). During the course of an interview their reflections on their biographies/experiences are both an interpersonal interaction and a performance to make connections to other persons with their stories. Similarly, online interviews constructed through text/speech acts are both an attempt by participants to connect with their text and to share this with a researcher. So interviews need sensitive handling by researchers especially when participants have difficult or sensitive stories to tell. This allows participants to feel cared for and/or have a sense of belonging while making sense of their experiences, as noted by a participant in Beck's study:

> It has taken me months to start to piece [things] together so I can understand what happened to me. This is one reason I have decided to try and write down my memories for this study, because I hope that writing things down in some logical 'order of events' will help me to find reasons for my random thoughts and feelings over this ... (Beck, 2005: 418)

Such interviews are 'contextual, immediate and grounded in the concreted specifics of the interactional situation' (Denzin, 1999: 112). However, the data emerging from them can be filled with misunderstandings, particular if the order of text is not the order of the dialogue. As Davis et al. (2004) highlighted in their research on HIV risk, turn-taking can be ambiguous in synchronous interviews. Although they used short, closed questions to foster simple question and answer sequences, the dialogue lost its single linear form and separated into more than one thread:

| Line 173: | <Interviewee> ye met a few bfs on here |
| 174: | <MD> all yr bfs? |
| 175: | <Interviewee> met some of my temps on here as well ☺ |
| 176: | <MD>wot is temp;-) |
| 177: | <Interviewee> no not all of my bfs |
| 178: | <MD> ok what made u go onto the internet |
| 179: | <Interviewee> bf's have come from various areas of life |
| 180: | <Interviewee> onto the net for sex you mean or just onto the net in general. (Davis et al., 2004: 949) |

While this interactional situation can provide another context in which turn-by-turn talk is re-engaged (Psathas, 1995, in Denzin, 1999), participants can depart from the turn-taking of questions and answers. Instead, as they can do in an unstructured face-to-face interview, participants can loop backwards and forwards to create the context for extended utterances such as stories and narratives (Denzin, 1999). In the fragmented context of online interviews, without the help of the non-visual cues normally present in face-to-face interviews, it is possible for researchers to misjudge when their participants have finished their answers (Bowker and Tuffin, 2005). The virtual world provides texts that emerge through but are also the substance of the performances and presentations made online, as discussed in Chapter 6.

Online interviews then can be viewed as a social performance (Atkinson and Silverman, 1997; Coffman, 1959), albeit mediated by the social and technical aspects of the Internet (Davis et al., 2004).

As we have argued in earlier chapters, synchronous interviews are useful for collecting factual information but seem less effective for researchers and participants to explore meanings in depth, when compared with asynchronous interviews that allow participants time to consider their responses carefully, rather than be confronted with the high level of immediacy that synchronous interviews can create (James, 2003). Such time for reflection also provides a 'safeguard' because participants are able to edit the text to convey the meanings they really intend (Mann and Stewart, 2000). For the researcher, too, there is more time to deliberate over the participants' reactions and consider a range of interpretations.

Nonetheless, whether such interviews are conducted in real-time or non-real-time, the data can only capture a snapshot of participants' lives and can disguise its evolving presence, as it produces data in material form (Jones, 1999). To supplement such data, researchers can use various forms of cyberethnography by not only observing the virtual setting, but asking questions and testing out ideas with participants to get a sense of the cultural context in which they have a part (Fox and Roberts, 1999).

The processes of online communities can be analysed as both text and speech (Hine, 2000) because communications are made up of text/speech acts. The texts from such conversations can be analysed as text alongside other documents derived from and relevant to the contexts of a study. However, they can also be analysed as interactions between participants, using conversation analysis to investigate the turns they take and the relationships they develop (Duncan-Howell, 2007). Discourse analysis can investigate the meanings and views participants may hold about changing social situations.

The textual aspects of an online community's exchanges can be analysed in various ways. Content analysis can be used for counting what topics are discussed and how frequently members of a community refer to them. Alternatively, the texts can be interrogated for emergent themes, investigating in a grounded manner what are the foci of participants' conversations. This approach can also be used to explore the discourses surrounding an online community that influence its members' actions. Another approach is to use critical textual analysis (Mitra and Cohen, 1999) to analyse the volume and content of text as well as what it says about the online community that has produced/consumed the text. It involves examining the:

- formality of the text and any significant features;
- way in which a single text is linked to other similar texts;
- role of the various readers who through reading the text, make it meaningful. (Mitra and Cohen, 1999: 182)

Investigations of 'intertextuality' explore how a variety of existing and past texts impinge on new texts (Mitra and Cohen, 1999: 181). One way to view this is that the present and 'here and now' of participants individually and in groups is constructed through the interactions of various texts that they write/speak and in which they are written. Online discourses, like offline discourses, need to be analysed in their contexts (Mulkay et al., 1983 in Hine, 2000: 122) in order to make sense of them.

The interactive aspects of the text/speech acts can be interrogated in various ways. Conversation analysis focuses on what participants say in what sequences (Psathas, 1995, in Denzin, 1999). It helps to reveal how the social networks of an online community operate. Questions of meanings can be referred back to the participants to clarify what they intended. This approach helps to explore the flows of power among participants by investigating how certain perspectives and voices emerge as dominant in the discourse of a community. 'The meaning of an action is given in the consequences produced by it, including the ability to explain past experience and predict future consequences' (Denzin, 1999: 110).

Critical discourse analysis (Doherty, 2007) investigates the meanings and flows of power perceived by different actors in the discourses of a particular community in and with the contexts in which it is located. Researchers need to examine the form of participants' interactions in terms of how meaningful utterances are directly/indirectly related to each other (Denzin, 1999). They also need to examine the contents of participants' interactions in terms of participants' identities, values and beliefs and the socio-political milieux they inhabit (Bourdieu, 1990).

Narrative analysis allows researchers to investigate how individuals construct the stories of themselves in particular contexts. James (2003) made extensive use of narrative analysis to probe the non-linearity of her participants' stories. The technical aspects of the Internet made it difficult for her to determine what was the authentic beginning of a participant's text in the asynchronous interviews she conducted. Participants' narratives did not have a specific structure that flowed from beginning to end. There was no progression in the reading of the text. This challenged conventional notions of narratives having a linear structure to them. Bowker and Tuffin (2004) found this when they conducted synchronous interviews using IRC. In these, the participant's responses tended to be made up of stilted phrases of very few words (see Chapter 2) and included incomplete and sometime incoherent sentences. The researchers had to continuously clarify their understanding of the discourse by reconstructing it with further explanations from participants. It seems that in the virtual space of online communication, codes of language and the logic of grammar become disconnected from the discrete elements of the text.

## Conclusion

This chapter has considered the complexities of the constructed cultures of online communities by discussing how they emerge through the interactions of their members in the third spaces of the Internet. Awareness of these complexities allows researchers to begin to address two important elements of their work. First, it allows them to consider how they might construct successful online research projects that are themselves online communities. In this the construction of collaborative cultures through the development of trust between researchers and participants is central. Second, it allows researchers to begin to consider how they might collect and analyse data from such online communities. However because of the nature of online communication through text/speech acts, such data can be analysed as both text and as interaction between participants. There are a variety of qualitative processes available to online researchers but some of these have to be adapted to suit the disembodied spaces of online interactions between people.

## Practical Tips for Online Researchers

- Use cultural artefacts in your communications with participants to signal the interpersonal values you want to create and sustain in your research.
- Acknowledge the complexity and hybridity of creating a small culture in an online research project.
- Acknowledge your peripherality when trying to join an existing online community for research purposes.
- Create trust through communicating openly, honestly, authentically and rapidly so as not to disrupt the online community.
- Listen carefully to participants' views and doubt your understandings of what they say.
- Read carefully the responses of your participants and wonder what they mean by their texts, especially if they have any unconventional features.

- Choose appropriate methods of data collection and analysis to answer the questions you have posed and explain this to participants.
- Consider how different texts of your participants relate to each other and to the contexts in which THEY are writing/speaking. Whose 'here and now' are you investigating?

## Further Reading

Day, G. (2006) *Community and Everyday Life*. Oxford: Routledge.

Howard, P.N. and Jones, S. (eds) (2004) *Society Online: The Internet in Context*. Thousand Oaks, CA: Sage Publications.

Schroeder, R. (ed.) (2002) *The Social Life of Avatars: Presence and Interaction in Shared Virtual Environments*. London: Springer.

# NINE

## Curating and Disseminating Online Qualitative Data

Overview: this chapter considers the general frameworks for curating data in qualitative research, before focusing on role of the online researcher in organising, storing, analysing and distributing data generated from online interviews. It also examines how issues related to the publication and dissemination of results can contribute to the dilemmas in deciding what is public and private data when research is conducted online.

### Introduction

Online research practice is still in its infancy so researchers are 'confronted by quandaries at almost every point in the research process' (Mann and Stewart, 2000: 8). One of these points is how data is stored or 'curated' (ESRC, 2005) and under what conditions. The safe curation and dissemination of data is an important aspect of a research project for researchers and other participants. It is, however, often a neglected topic.

This chapter is about the curation of data such as that generated from online interviews in qualitative research. It includes discussions on the actions that researchers might take to protect research project participants and their cultural artefacts from harm when research data is curated and published. Keeping participants from harm is part of the ethical framework of research which was discussed in Chapter 5. Research data not only has to be stored safely but also in a manner that allows legitimate scholars to access it to generate knowledge to benefit society. Consequently this chapter discusses how online researchers can organise, store, analyse and disseminate online qualitative data. There are various problems surrounding the curation of online text-based data. These are linked to the tensions that exist around what is considered public and private data. If online communication is considered to be in the public arena, participants and service providers could be held legally responsible for online messages (Madge, 2006).

## Curating Data

Researchers have to gather data and keep records during research projects (British Psychological Society [BPS], 2006). How this data is curated and published is informed by the moral precepts and ethical codes that were discussed in Chapter 5. These imply that 'where possible, threats to the confidentiality and anonymity of research data should be anticipated by researchers. The identities and research records of those participating in research should be kept confidential whether or not an explicit pledge of confidentiality has been given' (BSA, 2002: para. 35). However, it is preferable that researchers gain participants' informed consent to their data being stored and published in ways compatible with the purposes of a project. This requires researchers to remind 'potential informants and research participants, especially those possessing a combination of attributes that make them readily identifiable ... that it can be difficult to disguise their identity without introducing an unacceptably large measure of distortion into the data' (BSA, 2002: para. 36).

There are a number of aspects in the secure curation of data:

(i)   Keep 'personal information concerning research participants ... confidential. In some cases it may be necessary to decide whether it is proper or appropriate even to record certain kinds of sensitive information'. (BSA, 2002: para. 34)
(ii)  Collect and, therefore, store only data needed for the specific purposes of a research project. (ESRC, 2005)
(iii) Ensure the data collected for a project is not used in ways that 'are incompatible with the original purpose of the project'. (Elgesem, 2002: 201)
(iv)  Ensure that 'the form of any publication, including publication on the Internet, does not directly or indirectly lead to a breach of confidentiality and anonymity' (BERA, 2004: para. 26). This includes any agreements with third parties about the terms under which researchers are allowed access to data that has been collected already.

In Norway, the rules that apply to researchers' access to confidential material and those that apply to the storage of research material containing personal data are of especially great importance in respect of research. The public administration collects and stores large volumes of material that are generally subject to statutory confidentiality, but the law allows a certain right to grant exemptions from this confidentiality to allow researchers access to material. (NESH, 2006: para. 14)

How the appropriate curation and management of data is to be achieved may depend on the nature of the research project. Wood (2005) sets out some general principles of good practice which are shown in Box 9.1. These make clear how researchers need to preserve the anonymity of research participants. Research material should, 'normally be[ing] rendered anonymous, and the storage and destruction of lists of names or personal identity numbers must satisfy strict requirements' (Ess and the AoIR, 2002: 32: endnote 14). Further 'identifiers, the use of pseudonyms' should be removed and 'other technical means for breaking the link between data and identifiable individuals' (BSA, 2002: para. 36) be used.

## Box 9.1    Principles of good practice in data curation and management

- Data should be used for the purposes for which it has been collected and the purposes of the data clearly explained to participants.
- Data should be adequate and accurate and unnecessary data not collected.
- Personal data should not be kept longer than necessary and kept up-to-date as necessary.
- Personal data should not be disclosed to third parties.
- Data should not be unnecessarily reproduced in any form or left visible to third parties.
- Personal data should not be given over the telephone or email.
- No data relating to a specific individual should be disclosed to anyone unless permission has been granted.
- Personal data should be held securely and proper security measures taken for all methods of holding or displaying personal data to prevent loss, destruction, or corruption of information. (Adapted from Wood, 2005: 243–5)

It is often problematic for researchers to decide how long they should keep research project data after that project has finished. One view is that, 'data [is] not … stored any longer than what is needed to attain the objective for which it was processed' (NESH, 2006: para 16). The longer data is curated, particularly when linked to the personal data of participants, the greater the risk of inadvertent harm to the participants (ESRC, 2005). The risk increases further if the data is used for purposes other than the original research, even with the express permission of the original participants.

Conversely, bona fide researchers who wish to interrogate secondary data need to be able to have access to it. To make such access legitimate, the original researchers in a project 'must have participants' permission to disclose personal information to third parties' (BERA, 2004: para. 24). Further they must 'ensure that such parties are permitted to have access to the information. They are also required independently to confirm the identity of such persons and must keep a record of any disclosures' (BERA, 2004: para. 24). This is because the original researchers are responsible to their participants for preventing 'data being published or released in a form that would permit the actual or potential identification of research participants without prior written consent of the participants' (BSA, 2002: para. 36).

Tensions in the curation and dissemination of data can also emerge between researchers and other stakeholders in a project. The latter might be sponsors of research or gatekeepers of access to research sites. They have an interest in the intellectual property rights of the research outcomes and may have views in conflict with the findings of the research project. However it is important for researchers to protect their right to publish (Bulmer, 1988), so long as the identity of other stakeholders is protected by anonymity. So they should beware of giving a right of veto over what is published to gatekeepers of institutions or communities even if the latter have been willing hosts to a study.

Another site of tension in the curation of research project data is the rights of participants. In curating data researchers have to comply with two frameworks. One is the ethical codes that constrain their work. The other is the law of the nation state in which researchers are based. 'It is obviously the responsibility of researchers to be aware of the "most relevant acts of legislation" and make sure the processes of their research projects comply with them' (NESH, 2006: para. 14). However, this poses some particular problems where online researchers and participants are conducting cross-national research. Each person in the project needs to meet the data protection requirements of each country of which they are citizens.

In some countries the importance of protecting participants from harm when engaged in research or other online activities is reinforced by law. For example, in some countries Data Protection Acts define how important personal data collected and stored in an online environment can be used. In the USA there is a long and strong tradition of computer ethics (Capurro and Pringel, 2002) with which Europe is only just catching up. However, Europe, and particularly Germany, has a long tradition of protecting personal data. The state is supposed to play an important role as guarantor and provider of social equity (Capurro and Pringel, 2002).

In the UK, researchers must comply with the legal requirements for the storage and use of personal data as set down by the latest Data Protection Act 2003. People are entitled to know how and why their personal data is being stored, to what uses it is being put and to whom it may be made available' (BERA, 2004: para. 24). Consequently, researchers have to take 'appropriate measures … to store research data in a secure manner' BSA (2002: para. 36). In the USA the Freedom of Information Act to some extent plays a similar role in protecting the rights of citizens (Capurro and Pringle, 2002: 193). Researchers 'seeking to exploit legal exclusions to these rights must have a clear justification for so doing' (BERA, 2004: para. 25), particularly as many participants in a study want to know about the findings of a project in which they have some stake. One way for researchers to achieve this is to give their participants an account of the findings of the research (Sammons, 1989).

Another perspective on the rights of participants relates to what readers need to know about participants and their contexts if they are fully to understand the outcomes of the research. Embedded in this is a question about to what extent publishing details of participants or institutions in a research project might compromise their privacy. It implies that findings need to be reported in such a way that they are not open to misinterpretation. The writing up of research therefore has to be carried out ethically so that the presentation of the data both respects participants' right to privacy and sustains the right of society to know about the research (Burgess, 1989; Cohen et al., 2000).

## Curating and Disseminating Data from Online Research Projects

Curating online data poses its own particular problems for protecting the safety of participants. This is most obvious where data is stored on computers that are used by a variety of people, some of whom may not be part of a research project. This might include technical support staff in a large organisation. If non-members of a research project gain access to data they could leak details to other people or tamper with the data. For example, electronic records such as word processing files are very easy to alter unless they are held as read-only files. Even holding records as PDF files is no real deterrence. Users of text-based communication can manipulate messages stored on their own computers for retrieval, editing and sending to others (Kanayama, 2003).

In our studies, we had to think carefully about how to store interview data collected via email. In the first instance, we removed any identifiers (participants' names, geographical location and organisational affiliation) in the headers of the email, in order to render them anonymous. However, a concern for us was that our data was stored on networked computers that were backed up by our organisations' servers. 'The vast majority of computers in universities and places involved in research are networked to the internet, and as such are susceptible to attack from other internet users' (Fox et al., 2003: 179). While this ensured the data was unlikely to be lost – it was curated safely – it opened risks for the security of our data. Had the administrators backing up our data centrally wished to, they could have accessed our project data. Further, emails are retained on the server of the sending account, transmitting server and receiving server.

These issues can be particularly problematic, especially in online projects researching sensitive issues, for example, around drug taking or vulnerable people. There may be serious concerns that non-members of a project may want to gain access to data. The pressures on researchers are especially sharp if state authorities hold power to demand access to data held online, and are actively seeking information on the sensitive topics being researched. It faces researchers with questions about the appropriate medium to use for storing data or communicating with participants in such projects.

Researchers collecting online data can reduce the threat of non-members gaining access to data. The vignette overleaf illustrates how the research project tried to minimise this risk. Although the project was not an online project, it did collect a considerable amount of qualitative interview data electronically. Part of the project also involved participants taking photographs of their environment and their social networks on digital cameras. Such electronic data has the same properties as online qualitative data so needs to be curated in the same ways and with the same care. The project used un-networked laptop computers for data collection and storage for each site. The data from each computer was backed up on its own hard drive which was locked away in filing cabinets when not in use. Separate computers were used for each site to limit the number of people likely to come in to contact with the data from each site.

---

### Vignette: Curating data for a research project

This project investigates the views of staff and students about their communities and identities in the schools in which they work. Such views will also take account of the socio-political contexts in which teachers work. Two key aspects of the project are that participants will be asked to:

- contribute to the collection of data through the use of visual images and other media;
- comment on the social processes in which they take part in the school.

The anonymity and privacy of participants will be addressed by the ways in which the data collected during the project is stored and 'curated' and presented on websites, in reports and other publications. There are two main problems facing the collection, curation and dissemination of data in this project. The first is a political one. We are inviting staff and some students to comment on the interactions of groups of people and of themselves. This may raise contentious perspectives and be a source of stress. We will explicitly train and mentor school staff and students in how they can act ethically when presenting even contentious views in research using an evidence-based and non-personalised manner and guarding other people's privacy through protecting their anonymity.

The second is an ethical one. The collection, storage and ownership of data is problematic since qualitative and visual data make the identity of participants and other people instantly recognisable. To address this, we shall train the participants in the ethics of research as well as in the technicalities of acting as visual ethnographers. They, like the researchers, will have to gain permission from the potential subjects of their photographs, or take such measures as are necessary to protect the anonymity of persons caught on a photograph. Explicitly, in the UK, child protection legislation prevents photographs of children being taken without the consent of all associated parties including the students and parent(s)/guardian(s).

The curation of data poses long-term problems. Participants will be given an explanation of how photographs, taken as part of the project by project members, will be used in and after the project. This will form part of the process of gaining informed consent. To ensure that the storage of qualitative and visual data is secure, photographs and other qualitative data taken during the course of the project, at least during the lifetime of the project, will be kept in a locked filing cabinet or stored electronically on a password-protected external hard drive – one for each computer used by the project team. Where participants have taken photographs as part of the research project, i.e. it is a reflection of their 'work' and perspectives, we will allow them copyright of their own individual photographs, so long as they acknowledge the context of the research project in which the photographs were taken. However, where photographs taken by participants or other project staff are put together into collections for public display whether electronically (e.g. onscreen presentations; website material) or mechanically, the copyright of the collections will lie with the research project for the principal investigators.

In online interviews, data is generated as research conversations progress. The text that is generated can be stored online or copied into a word document to be manipulated later for data analysis. This applies equally to synchronous as to asynchronous interview data. In this facility also lies a risk that participants' anonymity and privacy will be compromised, even if inadvertently. As data is transformed from one medium to another, copies of it may become lodged in insecure environments, as is discussed below. This can make participants' views instantly visible.

Participants in online spaces do not always perceive their communications as public, and actually carry with them the expectation of privacy, especially in chat rooms (Bassett and O'Riordan, 2002). Researchers' early and comprehensive appreciation of the potential threats to participants' privacy in a research project is at the heart of protecting participants from these, especially when working with participants in isolated geographical regions or with limited economic resources. Some participants may not own a computer but have to use one in a public space such as a library or an Internet café. This may affect the quality of the data collected. For example, in discussing sensitive topics, participants may not want to display personal content on a computer screen where others can see it. Despite efforts to protect anonymity of online communication with data encryption and other security features, participants may be concerned that the sensitive or personal data they share with the online researcher might be obtained by others and used against them (Mathews and Cramer, 2008). However, encryption only works if all participants use the same email software that shares the same encryption capabilities (Mann and Stewart, 2000: 43). The issue is compounded by hackers potentially being able to access such data, especially if stored on computer files. Such issues make it difficult for researchers to guarantee that stored data is secure and will not be accessed and used by others.

Researchers must then decide 'how to approach their projects and thus where to locate themselves in terms of the groups or audiences whose perspectives they will consider' (McKee and Porter, 2008: 21). One way is to require participants to communicate anonymously with researchers. However, this anonymity is easy to breach. For example, if participants chose to use email as well as a project website to communicate with researchers, then the anonymity afforded by the website is compromised by identification given by the email address (Fox et al., 2003). This is because email addresses contain elements that make them traceable back to the embodied participants. This problem can be addressed by using a dedicated bulletin-board linked to a project to allow participants to communicate with researchers anonymously (Fox et al., 2003), unless they sign their messages with their real name!

Online procedures for curating data and anonymising participants can be complex where the original data is routinely made available to other participants. If discussions in online focus groups include the headers of a message then participants can become identifiable as outlined in the discussion thread:

> Remy:}[<—notice distinctive mark … others recognise me by this. Many of us know each other so well that even with removing sexual etc. inferences in our speech, we can still figure out who it is. In my case, I have found that few recognise me without my smiley face at the end of sentences. Other personal marks such as my constant typo of remeber instead of remember and … long run on sentences etc … styles, are almost impossible to completely disguise and still be able to reply to our own words. Is anonymity to protect us?].
> (Williams, 2003, in Stewart and Williams, 2005: 412)

Another approach is by using participant pseudonyms or fictitious but identifying names in computer-mediated communications. One means of doing this is to use an intermediary in a research project. The intermediary might, for example, allocate numbers to participants using a random number generator and only allow the researchers to identify the participants by those numbers. The list of names and pseudonyms could be locked in a secure safe away from the research project. Alternatively, researchers could require their participants to use a fake email name. Hessler et al. (2003) stored all communications with each participant under that fake email name to ensure that somebody seeking a participant's identity would be unable to do so. Online pseudonyms 'function for most purposes just like real names, and should be treated the same way' (Bruckman, 2002a: 229). So using them is unlikely to damage the quality of interaction between participants and researchers. However, the nature of 'disguise' will depend on the research project, and the ethical philosophical stance of the researcher.

Online data needs to be protected from other people tampering with or accessing it. It is important to ensure that data is not curated in the same filing system as the identifying information of participants. Password protecting computer files, saving anonymised data and participants' identifying information separately (Kraut et al., 2004) or coding data in such a way to ensure that it is not traceable back to a specific participant (Pittinger, 2003) offers ways to protect participants. However, if these systems are cross-referenced it becomes relatively easy to match participants identifying information to their anonymised data files. Where such information and data are stored on the same site – or in the same files! – it becomes very easy for researchers, or somebody else wishing to do so, to match the (anonymous) participants' views to their physical world selves. This will breach participants' anonymity and risk causing them harm. For example, reducing the use of email, and setting up a discussion thread on a research website may alleviate the problem (Fox et al., 2003). However, if the email and web-based data of a project are stored together, the anonymity afforded by the website will be breached. A similar problem arises when a hard copy consent form, bearing a participant's name and address, is referenced to electronic qualitative data stored anonymously (Hessler et al., 2003). Researchers need to make choices about what categories of data in a research project should be stored together, and what types of (online) communication should be used for particular research projects depending on the sensitivity of the topics being investigated.

Perhaps the picture of data insecurity is not so bleak as the foregoing may suggest. 'The growing use of commercial accounts for online interaction makes it difficult to catch the participants' identity cues' (Lee, 2006: 9). The increasing amount of re-mailing makes it almost impossible for a receiver to breach a sender's privacy. When data collected through re-mailing is stored with its headers on it is unlikely to lead to a research participants' anonymity being unmasked. Indeed, Lee (2006) reports the difficulty he had in tracking down a participant who dropped out of his research because his Internet communications had provided so very little information about either his online or offline identity.

### Private World/Public World?

Guidance on the dissemination and publication of online research data is not clear cut. In part this is because the division between the private world and the public world of an individual is blurred in online communications and people experience a sense of a loss of control over who is able to read their private conversations (Bakardjieva and Feenberg, 2000). Nevertheless: 'Who owns a message posted to a chat room discussion?' (Madge, 2006). In online worlds, the possibilities of not only recording, but also reproducing and analysing online data covertly cannot be ignored. If this world is perceived public then researchers can freely quote and analyse online information if:

- It is officially and publicly archived.
- No password is required for archived access.
- No site policy prohibits it.
- The topic is not highly sensitive. (Bruckman, 2002b)

Adopting this approach raises challenges for the researcher as the following vignette illustrates.

This vignette suggests that the online environment can be viewed as a public space, one in which online participants make a choice to communicate and accept that anybody can have access to data that emerges from that communication. In this view, researchers are external to those being researched and are interested in the:

> … generation and transmission of plentiful data, and not community facilitation or civil transformation. This approach centralises the research project. Decisions regarding the conduct of the research are made by the researchers based on these concerns. (Chen et al., 2004: 173)

However, this exacerbates the potential problems and risks of disseminating research project data in a way that protects participants from harm. In this open environment there may be people who are in a position to recognise some of the participants in a study or the site of a study, or who want to make malicious use of the information they gain from research reports. Even when researchers have used pseudonyms when writing about participants, institutions or websites, sometimes those pseudonyms are traceable back to the original participants. For example, pseudonyms may contain references to obvious features of online or physical sites related to participants, potentially revealing their embodied identity. Where participants have adopted pseudonyms, rather than being ascribed them by researchers, they may be revelatory of participants' identities because they have been used by them in other (online) contexts.

Conversely, if online research conversations are in the private rather than the public domain of communication, researchers need to be particularly careful in curating and disseminating data to avoid harm to participants. As noted earlier, participants in online research regard their conversations as private even when they are posting on an open website that can be accessed quite easily by outsiders (Sharf, 1999). The more sensitive the topics being researched the greater the need for care. The data is, after all, a part of the participants' selves. This is especially important when online research projects involve communities/groups. In this case, researchers could adopt a collaborative approach to collecting and disseminating data. Their goals then would be 'not to generate or transmit plentiful data but to inform the community, as well as to interpret the community to others outside' (Chen et al., 2004: 173). One way to do this would be to engage the participants throughout the research process in the process of proto-dissemination. This could be achieved by researchers creating a common area on a project website where researchers could post emerging analysis and participants could post their responses. This in turn could shape the direction of the research (Mathews and Cramer, 2008).

Two implications emerge from this. One is that researchers should make their intentions for publication clear to participants when they request consent at the start of a project. The second is that if researchers want to publish in ways not covered by participants' original consent then they need to seek further consent for this. Further, if researchers are using data sets from other projects as secondary sources for their own work, they, too, need to gain the consent of the original participants before publishing material from them. This is particularly so given the growth in the commercial interests of the Internet.

## Conclusion

There is no solution (Burgess, 1989: 8)! It is now difficult for researchers to anticipate how online data might be (re)used and by whom. Further, harm is inherent to all research, and the uncertainty over whether any action will cause harm is a fact of all qualitative research' (Baez, 2002: 53). The ethical issues and practical problems surrounding the curation and dissemination of online data are 'related to the special features of online communications' (Elgesem, 2002: 201). This is because 'fieldwork is inherently problematic by virtue of the conditions that make knowledge production possible … where personal relations and social interactions are the context for unearthing meaning' (de Laine, 2000: 205).

The trend towards using the Internet for data collection purposes means that the role of the researcher as custodian and gatekeeper of online project data has altered. Ultimately, online researchers have to take decisions about how to curate and disseminate data in as careful a manner as possible within the frameworks of the project, including its budgets of time and finance. However, they also need to be aware of any actions that might create unintended consequences for their participants in the publication and dissemination of data (Mathews and Cramer, 2008). These include weighing up the balance of harm and benefit that arise to participants and to society from collecting, curating and publishing project data. On balance it may be deemed unacceptable to store some data or to publish others. One approach is to treat participants who write and post texts as authors who require acknowledgement for their work in the form of direct citation, permission and explicit attribution (Ess, 2004). In this way, online material will be *prima facie* protected by copyright law (Bassett and O'Riordan, 2002). This highlights how researchers are not always 'autonomous self-directing actors' but mediators between two or more audiences (de Laine, 2000: 205).

Online research creates a further set of challenges for researchers trying to ensure the truthfulness and trustworthiness of the outcomes of a project. These challenges, alongside the absence of a commonly agreed set of codes of practice, suggest that researchers have many difficult decisions to make if the publications from their research are to be fit for purpose. One of these decisions will be how to convince participants and potential participants that no harm will come to them from taking part in a research project. A major aspect of that is likely to be in persuading participants that their data will be stored safely and their views disseminated responsibly by the researchers when they publish the findings of a research project. Perhaps for many participants two key aspects of that responsible publication will be the benefits that the research will bring to others and the lack of harm that it will do to themselves.

From the foregoing discussion, and from other sources, it may be possible to construct a set of guidelines to make the curation and dissemination of data from online research projects more secure and more accessible. This is shown in the following practical tips for online researchers.

## Practical Tips for Online Researchers

- Recognise the potential risks to participants before you start your project.
- Consider exactly what data you need to collect from participants and what data you do not need to achieve the purposes of your project.
- Consider the likely impact on participants of some of the project data being made public accidentally and take appropriate action to avoid that happening.
- Construct a safe environment for collecting and storing data, using a dedicated project website if necessary/possible.
- Ensure that data collected anonymously is not stored with information about participants since this could allow the anonymous data to be attributed to particular participants.
- Jettison/destroy any unnecessary data that you have collected, even if inadvertently.
- Consider and discuss with participants how they will be (re)presented in the project report.
- Check that the privacy and data security constructed is adequate for the research.

## Further Reading

Bruckman, A. (2002) 'Studying the amateur artist: a perspective on disguising data collected in human subjects research on the Internet', *Ethics and Information Technology* 4 (3): 217–31.

Nosek, B., Baaji, M. and Greenwald, A. (2002) 'E-research: ethics, security, design and control in psychological research on the Internet', *Journal of Social Issues* 58 (1): 161–76.

Sikes, P. (2006) 'On dodgy ground? problematics and ethics in educational research', *International Journal of Research and Method in Education,* 29 (1): 105–17.

# TEN

## Conclusion

Overview: the Internet presents online researchers with many challenges and possibilities. This chapter pulls together the practical implications raised throughout the previous discussions in this book. It considers how online researchers might tackle the epistemological and methodological challenges and opportunities facing them in the construction of online interviews. The chapter also discusses how online researchers might cope with the ethical and political processes which surround them. It also indicates how they can surmount the cultural and personal conundrums of creating trustworthy online conversations. The chapter concludes by considering how to construct collaborative research cultures to facilitate participants' engagement in online research projects.

### Introduction

The emergence of the Internet in the late 20th century as a means of mass communications has had a significant impact on people's social interactions and the ways in which they conduct their lives. The Internet has provided opportunities for individuals to meet a wider range of people in different places from those they could normally access easily face-to-face. It has allowed them to communicate for business and cultural purposes at a speed that would not have been possible before. It has realised the emergence of a 'there and now' to complement people's usual lived experiences of the 'here and now' (Zhao, 2006). In so doing, the Internet has challenged people's understandings of what it means to be part of a community and how communities are constructed, especially when they are located in the warped time/space of online communications.

However, not everybody in the world has equal access to the Internet. Many people lack access to computer equipment, software, electricity or even the literacy skills needed to use the Internet effectively (Janelle and Hodges, 2000). These people are often economically disadvantaged and are then further disadvantaged by not being able to access the information available on and through the Internet (Evans, 2004). The problem is compounded because the processes and conventions of the Internet are heavily influenced by American/Western culture and the dominant language of the Internet is

English (Jankowski and van Selm, 2005). This puts non-native speakers of English who are not familiar with the American/Western cultural precepts at a disadvantage when using the Internet. For researchers, it raises uncomfortable questions about the nature of the cultural context and how people can participate in an online research project. Almost certainly the poorer people in various societies, as well as those in less wealthy countries, are much more difficult to reach online than richer people in affluent societies.

As the Internet has spread, it has become popular as a medium for research. Initially colonised by market researchers and other people wanting to carry out online surveys with populations distant from the researcher's base, more recently qualitative social science researchers have begun to realise its possibilities. One of the more obvious ways of doing this is to use the Internet to carry out structured or semi-structured interviews with participants living at a distance, including different nation states, from the researchers. The Internet opens up the possibility of researchers being able to carry out international research using qualitative interview methods without the time and expense of having to go overseas. Another possibility now emerging is that of using the properties of the Internet to allow researchers to construct unstructured interviews with participants (James, 2003). This allows participants to develop, at length and in depth, their narratives of their engagement with particular situations.

If the Internet provides a medium through which various social science research methods can be deployed, it also provides a range of sites that social scientists can investigate. The growth of the Internet has spawned a wide variety of communities and networks for social, administrative and business purposes. These virtual communities have particular dynamics which alter as well as mimic the normal processes of face-to-face social exchange. The interfaces between such virtual communities and their members' offline physical, social and political lives are also topics of considerable interest. How researchers enter these sites and cope with the contexts of interactions they encounter, and construct productive means of engaging in research with members of these communities is critical to the final outcomes of a research project.

This chapter brings together the ethical, methodological and epistemological challenges and possibilities that researchers are presented with when using online interviews to collect qualitative data. In doing so, it will also consider the use of the Internet for online research projects more generally, and the practical implications.

## Epistemological and Methodological Challenges and Opportunities for Researchers

The construction of knowledge in online qualitative research is related to the philosophical underpinnings that researchers choose. The interpretive research perspective assumes that the human world is constructed by its inhabitants, rather than being dependent on immutable natural laws. This leads to various practical approaches for researchers. First, it leads researchers to choose single sites, be they communities, institutions or practices, for research investigation. If participants in a situation construct the social processes of a site then what they construct is unlikely to be the same as what participants on another site might construct. So a researcher might investigate two or more sites to make a comparison but is unlikely to carry out a survey across sites. The latter might presuppose that people on different sites will act in a similar fashion given similar conditions, which contradicts the prior assumption that people co-construct their world in the circumstances in which they find themselves.

Second, it leads researchers to find out the views of as many participants in a situation as they can, since each participant is likely to have a different perspective of the situation being investigated by the researchers. Researchers using qualitative methods draw on the interplay of the multiple views and voices of participants in a situation to construct knowledge of the dynamics of that situation; they have the ability to search for a deeper understanding of participants' lived experiences (Illingworth, 2006).

However, it is important for researchers to establish the authenticity of their participants' perspectives since the trustworthiness of the outcomes of the research depend on this. If that trustworthiness is damaged then the research can be useless, representing a waste of resources, including the time of the participants and the researchers. Researchers need to be convinced that the views expressed by participants are their own and reflect their lived experiences in the situation being discussed. They also need to be convinced that the views expressed are minimally contaminated by participants' thoughts about how they should present themselves to meet their understandings of the researchers.

Third, it raises questions about the nature of the relationship to be constructed between researchers and participants. In this perspective on the construction of knowledge, participants and researchers work together to construct understandings of the situations in which participants are living and working. Researchers are not trying to excavate knowledge from participants that they can then analyse in whatever ways help them to test the theories they hold about a particular aspect of human activity or behaviour. Participants, as co-constructors of knowledge of the situations which they inhabit, are also co-constructors of the analysis of the knowledge about a situation which emerges during the course of a research project.

In this approach to the construction of knowledge (epistemology), participants are co-owners of it with the researchers who are carrying out the investigations. A major practical implication of this is that participants are entitled to receive copies of publications from a project. They also have an entitlement over the use of the knowledge constructed with the researchers during a research project. For this reason it is essential that researchers consult and gain the consent of participants about the ways in which data from a project may be used during and after the lifetime of a project.

In qualitative research projects, researchers have to consider not only the epistemology that guides their research approach, but also the methodology to be chosen. In the last 10 years or so, it has become possible for researchers using qualitative methods to expand their methodological horizons. One aspect of this has been for researchers to design research projects to investigate the activities of participants living at a distance from them using research methods tailored to the technology of the Internet. Conventional qualitative research interviews such as individual interviewing, group interviewing and focus groups have been adapted for the Internet and used asynchronously and synchronously. These methods can collect in-depth and contextually situated data in the online setting (Mann and Stewart, 2000). They can produce both reflective narratives and more spontaneous responses.

Another aspect has been for researchers to use cyberethnography to investigate the processes of online communities. Researchers' participation in such communities can be constructed through participant observation and synchronous or asynchronous interviews as well as through the more ethically dubious process of lurking in chat rooms and MUDs (Markham, 1998). Lurking challenges researchers to decide whether or not it is necessary to their projects and how they can justify it ethically. Lurking may be a necessary first step for researchers choosing an appropriate site or social network to research (Chen et al., 2004). However, having made that choice, ethical guidelines (e.g. Ess and the AoIR, 2002) suggest researchers must make clear to members of a community their identity and purpose in wanting to become members of a site.

Engagement with online participants in research projects requires researchers to be clear about their aims and research design and how these play out in the cultural contexts in which their participants are embedded. This means thinking carefully about how a rigorous research methodology can be constructed online to generate trustworthy outcomes from a project. It is important for researchers to provide participants with clear justification for the methodology of a project and the research methods, such as online interviews, that they want to use. They also need to explain how they are going to use these methods to collect, analyse and curate data.

So, if researchers are going to transfer commonplace qualitative research methods to the online environment they need to work out how they are going to do this and pilot their approach. For example, what actually does a semi-structured interview look like when it is transferred to an asynchronous process in the attenuated time and space of the Internet? How can a focus group discussion be conducted online, perhaps in a VLE? What might be the impact on the quality of discussion if a group interview is run synchronously or asynchronously as a moderated web-board discussion? What constitutes overt participant or non-participant observation in an online community? How can blogs be used as online diaries for participants in a study?

The use of the Internet for interviews depends on the willingness of participants to use this medium. In part, this may be linked to the myths and fears people hold about the Internet, as well as the practicalities about their ease of access to it or their familiarity with it. The Internet can provide researchers with the potential to cross geographical dimensions, but cultural, legal and linguistic limitations mean that identifying and recruiting hard to reach populations may be a challenge for researchers (Mathews and Cramer, 2008). The digital divide means that online research can be very geographically and socially excluding. Online interviews may well then include sample bias, and be non-representative of large parts of the global population.

The use of the Internet for research may limit whom researchers 'speak' to and whose lives they engage with especially in certain communities/cultures. People in one country participating in an online interview may interpret ideas and questions presented by a researcher differently to the intended meaning. For example, what constitutes an appropriate mode of address to a person in one culture may be considered unacceptable in another. Participants and researchers might make different uses of the language of communication in a research project. Participants and researchers could use English words in subtly different ways causing them to partially misunderstand each other. This problem not only comes from the different cultural backgrounds that researchers and participants inhabit but also depends on whether or not they are native speakers of English. So when starting a research project, researchers need to explore their participants' cultural understandings of Internet communication and their hopes and fears of it. Researchers can help to allay participants' fears by constructing a safe and supportive online environment, perhaps by using a dedicated website for a project.

The time zones that participants in a research project inhabit affect the ways in which researchers might choose to undertake their research. So it is important for researchers to establish in which time zones their participants are located and how this affects their accessibility to the Internet. Researchers are likely to get better quality data if they can interact with their participants at times convenient to the participant. For example, synchronous interviews may be difficult with participants living more than eight hours apart from a researcher. The prolonged periods of participant reflection and re-statement during the social interaction of asynchronous online interviews can allow time for both distance and reflection.

Asynchronous online communication enables researchers and (groups of) participants that are separated in time and space to engage in the active production of shared knowledge. It has the further benefit of supporting 'the co-construction of knowledge through discourse' (Gilbert and Dabbagh, 2005: 6). Making space for participants' discourses is important, but researchers also need to consider the significance of the context of those discourses, in terms of 'how' and 'where' (Illingworth, 2006). It is this temporal and spatial element of online interviewing that can be lost, and yet is an important part of the interview process. In online interviews, in many cases, researchers do not know where the participants are, when they reply or under what circumstances, unless participants tell them.

One aspect of research design that is peculiar to online research, and has been widely debated among the Internet research community, is whether an online interview should have an offline component. Researchers' stance on this reflects their views on the epistemology of their projects. Researchers need to make choices about whether an offline component is necessary for a project, perhaps to strengthen the study's claims of authenticity or trustworthiness. They should not assume that triangulating online research with offline contexts and face-to-face interactions will ensure truthfulness and candour. Further, online and offline interviews are different types of discourses and need to be analysed with this in mind (Orgad, 2005).

Researchers therefore need to decide whether an offline component is essential for establishing positive relationships with participants. If they and their participants meet physically during other aspects of their lives, researchers need to decide how they might make positive use of contacts to further their online research. If researchers hold the view that what happens 'online is interwoven with offline social life and that the two are mutually shaped and shaping' (Hine, 2004) then they need to establish the nature of their online interaction. Previous discussion in this book has highlighted a range of strategies that researchers can use to ensure that data collected from online research interviews is authentic in its own right, rather than using face-to-face interviews to verify that data. The stronger and more positive interpersonal relationships that researchers build online with their participants the more likely they are to generate an authentic dialogue with them. One means of doing this is to allow participants to shape the process of the online interviews, perhaps modifying the rules of engagement about when and how frequently participants can post responses to researchers' questions. Another is for researchers to allow research conversations to contain elements of personal discussion from time to time, albeit while ensuring that they achieve their research agenda. This last process could involve researchers being willing to share aspects of their personal life, where relevant, with participants.

Researchers can also encourage participants to take greater ownership of a research project by co-constructing its values with the researcher. In this process, participants can also become responsible for the cultural reproduction of a research study, in which they have a part, and so a stronger investment in ensuring that the outcomes of that study are credible and authentic. This involves the engagement of researchers and participants in a process of collaboration and social negotiation in which it is possible to share experiences and reflect on what they know.

## Political and Ethical Challenges and Opportunities for Researchers

When research is conducted in the online environment, researchers need to re-examine closely their research practice. Online research can entail greater risks to participants' privacy and confidentiality, and for the researcher, greater challenges in assuring participants' identities or the trustworthiness of data. Ethical procedures and cultural frameworks can play a part in supporting online researchers to design and conduct 'ethical research'. However, there is a need for researchers to take responsibility and to reflect critically in each online project they conduct.

In constructing online research projects researchers using qualitative methods cannot assume that their participants can speak freely on the Internet. They need to be aware of the legal and less legal means of scrutiny to which their participants' communications might be subjected. Nor may there be any widely supported norms in many countries about how people's communications on the Internet might be used by third parties. This will affect the way in which participants are able to communicate with them. Many countries screen the content of Internet communication or spy on its contents. This can be in spite of or within the framework of international agreements on the use of the Internet.

The way in which the researcher and participant(s) enter the online setting, and communicate is critical for the research process. Researchers are in very powerful positions when they establish research projects and invite participants to join them. Entering the online setting requires an effective interaction between 'structuredness, [a]synchronous communication and the constructivist process of meaning ...' (Gilbert and Dabbagh, 2005: 7–8). To do this, researchers must gain the informed consent of participants. They also need to make both the purpose of the project and the security of its environment visible to participants. These approaches reinforce an ethic of care by the researcher providing clear guidelines or rubrics about how the online interview should be operationalised in order to aid the development of meaningful discourse. This is important whether the interview is one-to-one and conducted by email, or an online discussion group.

However, participants also have power in the construction and implementation of online research projects. They can fully engage in the interview, asking questions and reflecting back in the interaction or simply withdraw without any notification of their intentions to do so. This methodology allows participants to take greater ownership of discourses as they can return to it, and expand on/clarify their ideas and redefine phenomena. In this sense, 'it is not the researcher who is in the position to have the final word; the interpretation remains open to constant re-negotiation by both the researcher and researched' (Ward, 1999). Further, when researchers want to join an existing online community, members of it, who may be potential research participants, have the power to allow or not allow a researcher to join that community.

One aspect of research design in which researchers have responsibility is in constructing a project environment in which it is safe for participants to express themselves. So, before setting up a project, researchers have to consider how to construct a safe environment in which they and their participants can work. They also have to consider how safe an online environment they need to construct to meet the purposes of their research project. Their decisions about this are likely to relate to the aims of their project. Projects dealing with sensitive topics or vulnerable people are likely to need very secure environments, whilst projects dealing with matters that are generally part of common debate are less likely to do so.

If research is not carried out ethically then it is unlikely to be trustworthy because it will be very difficult to authenticate the data gathered and analysed. So it is very important for researchers to carry out their work in an ethical manner in accordance with the various codes of practice available for social scientists working in online environments. The variety of ethical codes, alongside a range of approaches to online research interviews (as well as other research methods), highlight how online research varies according to different methodologies and virtual contexts (Madge, 2007: 666). The absence of explicit practical and ethical guidelines on the conduct of Internet research should not be used as an excuse for researchers to do whatever they want.

In online worlds, the possibilities of not only recording, but also reproducing and analysing online data covertly cannot be ignored. The environment of a research project includes the processes for storing/curating interview data securely and publishing its findings without causing harm to its participants. One aspect of this is that researchers must decide how to protect the privacy of their participants and their institutions. Another is for researchers to consider and make clear to participants exactly what data they need to collect to achieve the purposes of their project. Collecting and storing unnecessary data might lead to participants' identities being revealed accidentally. For example, if data collected anonymously is stored with information about participants it could allow the anonymous data to be attributed to particular participants. It can also lead to unnecessary amounts of participants' time being used. Such a waste of resources is itself unethical.

There is still much ambiguity about the use and scrutiny of data constructed and curated in an online medium. AUPs as well as data protection and privacy laws can protect participants and ensure that data stored on a computer has adequate security. Researchers too must ensure that their online research practice involves an ethic of respect for their participants; that they do not endanger their participants in any way nor risk jeopardising the outcomes of their research project. Ethical considerations in online research should be a reflexive process that takes account of codes of conduct relating to both behaviour in computer-mediated communication and the practice of social research (Stewart and Williams, 2005: 410).

## Constructing Collaborative Research Cultures

Since the last decade of the 20th century, online technology has provided a communication network through which individuals can establish virtual communities (Rheingold, 1994). In these, people come together for some purpose, connect with each other and create shared values and cultures which may or may not democratise participation. The social structures and modes of communication that people create are specific to different social groups (Bishop, 2006; Joinson, 2005). The Internet, then, provides an environment in which people can create cultural contexts filled with rich and complex social experiences (Hine, 2000).

The establishment of online communities has opened up the possibilities of researchers using interviewing techniques to engage in 'natural' as opposed to contrived research settings. Using ethnographic processes researchers can observe participants in the field or site where social action takes place (Lincoln and Guba, 1985; Mann and Stewart, 2000). Leaving aside the question of lurking, researchers need to construct means of entering such communities. As with the construction of online research communities, there seems to be a strong argument for researchers to be honest about who they are and why they want to join a community. Not only is it much easier for people to sustain authentic stories of themselves that are closely related to their real world selves, but it also forestalls any problems should researchers and (some) participants meet offline. Being honest seems to help members of online communities to accept researchers into them, particularly where researchers are willing to play a minor but active role in posting to a community as a member. It helps community members to recognise the authenticity of the researcher.

An important element in accessing the field is for researchers to adopt appropriate language. At one level this means not only learning how members of an online community use language but also researchers demonstrating that they, too, can use it properly. This process can be seen as one of becoming literate in the processes of a community by listening and observing the text/speech acts of members as well as talking/posting to an online community (Kress, 2000). At another level it means using the lingua franca of an online community, be it English or some other language, skilfully. Researchers need to adapt their use of language to the competence of the other members of a community to help members understand what they mean as well as to understand the meanings constructed by the participants. This process of using language appropriately is equally important in constructing research projects online, whether using synchronous or asynchronous communications.

The use of appropriate language by researchers when entering online communities helps them to indicate that they are adopting as well as adapting to the culture of group. In the text/speech acts of online communications researchers can use cultural artefacts to signal the interpersonal values they want to create and sustain in their research. This could as easily be complimenting somebody for being punctual in responding to a question as being empathetic to somebody who has been delayed in posting because of pressures of work.

However, it also means developing an empathetic understanding of the ways in which people use or manipulate the surface features of language in online text/speech acts. Researchers should enquire of participants what they mean by the ways in which they (re)use conventional language signs in new ways in online communication. This happens because written/typed language is the only means of communicating online. There are no visual or non-verbal clues to help as there are in face-to-face communication. So people invent new ways of using language signs to convey more subtle shades of meaning.

Being responsive to participants' views also helps to establish a particular culture in a research project. In part this can happen by researchers carefully listening/reading participants' views and doubting what they have heard/seen, that is, asking supplementary questions. This expression of interest in the person of the participant, especially if it appears to stray from the line of questioning set up a by a researcher, helps participants to believe that the researcher is genuinely interested in them rather than just in collecting data. The same approach works equally well in face-to-face interviews!

Being responsive to participants also takes the form of researchers replying quickly to participants' comments and questions at any stage in the research. Some of these questions may be about simple administrative matters, such as when is the next question going to be sent by the researcher. Others might be about researchers' points of view on some topic. This indicates that researchers need to be realistic in setting the time frame for questioning and responding to participants when they are constructing their project. As discussed earlier, it also indicates the importance of researchers carefully thinking through the processes of a project, so it can be explained to participants, before starting a project.

Collaborative research cultures help participants to engage with researchers using qualitative online interviews,, in the most productive ways possible. A major element in constructing this culture is by making participants feel as comfortable, safe and valued as possible. Participants can also be involved in some of the decision-making processes of a project. Researchers can consult them about how and how quickly they want to respond to questions. Even simple matters such as inviting participants to indicate how they prefer to be addressed and named in a project can help to make participants feel more engaged. This is how researchers can show their respect for participants as people rather than just as sources of data.

Researchers can enhance collaborative cultures by inviting participants to become co-owners of a research project so that they have a stake in it and its outcomes. Researchers can develop this sense by allowing participants to have some control over the process and direction of conversations. Such new agenda items in the research can be nested alongside the original agenda of a project. In online research studies this is unlikely to distort the outcomes of a project that seeks to make sense of participants' understandings of a particular situation.

Another aspect of co-ownership is for researchers to acknowledge to participants that they have interests in a project and in its outcomes. These interests might take the form of altruistic benefits, for example, the project is intended to benefit communities/society. They might take the form of more material benefits, for example participants gain new knowledge or develop a self-identity as a valued person in a project; this can be supported by researchers acting in a respectful manner to participants. The enactment of co-ownership helps researchers to authenticate their emerging understandings of the social situation being investigated.

## Conclusion

Developments in computer-mediated communication continue to shape the way in which individuals interact and, in turn, the way in which research is carried out on the Internet. Technological advances in online interviewing also have the potential to 'provide an opportunity for interrogating and understanding methodological commitments' (Hine, 2005: 9). They can provide a useful approach to investigating the social realities of everyday life from an individual perspective as well as provide 'a research window into understanding the contemporary negotiation of the ... project of the self in late/postmodern times' (Hookway, 2008: 107).

In the 21st century, the Internet does not have to simply reply on text-only communication. The capacity to increase voice and video communication is evident in the development of social networking sites such as Facebook, and in the use of blogs (see, for example, Hookway, 2008; Phippen, 2007). In addition, the availability of high quality voice and video applications using Skype in which it is possible to talk, chat or make video calls, and Voice over Internet Protocol (VoIP) that allows voice communications using IP networks means that it is possible to conduct online interviews face-to-face using video links and voice-chat software between computers. Videoconferencing can be used for the conduct of qualitative interviews, including the possibility for researchers to utilise voice recognition software to create rough transcripts of interviews to refine/develop interview guides or prompting questions (Mathews and Cramer, 2008: 307). All this technology offers researchers innovative approaches to online interviewing in social research, but as yet remain relatively unexamined as methods of qualitative data collection in the social sciences. It moves researchers away from the question and answer format common to conventional interviewing conventions. They can allow more than one voice to speak, and the text can now include discourse, character, voice, tone and visual imagery. This in turn provides researchers with a new space and dimension in which participants can explore who they are and what they think they know. Such developments also indicate the need for researchers to establish their online research practice, rather than adapting face-to-face research methods for the virtual world. In turn, researchers can begin to research and better understand the epistemological, methodological and ethical implications of the Internet in its own right.

'There is no closure' (Derrida in Wolfreys 1998), only endless new possibilities to be debated as one understanding is constructed after another. However, in such 'moments of innovation' researchers need to be critically reflexive in their practice (Hine, 2005: 9). The decision to use online research needs to be based on 'an evaluation of the respective advantages and disadvantages in relation to the specific topic that is to be investigated' (Denscombe, 2003: 41). The use of online interviews in qualitative research (as well as other online research methods) should not be seen as an easy option. Researchers need to justify the use of the Internet to conduct their research and indeed what benefits it can bring to their research projects. The effectiveness of online research interviews is dependent on who is being researched, what is being researched and why. The use of the Internet to conduct online interviews in qualitative research comes with a set of epistemological, methodological and ethical considerations and tensions as we have discussed throughout this book. But it also offers exciting possibilities!

# Glossary

**Asynchronous/non-real-time** communication takes place at a different time, same place

**Blog** an online diary to which other 'bloggers' can post comments in a public forum

**Cyberspace** refers to the digital world and is a field of interaction, existing in a independent reality separate from offline environments, bodies and concerns

**Community of practice** 'a set of relations among persons, activity, and world, over time and in relation to other tangential and overlapping communities of practice' (Lave and Wenger, 1991: 98)

**Curation** looking after data when it has been collected and making it available for legitimate/ethical use

**Cyberethnography** the study of online interactions displays and performances/physical and virtual realms that are inseparable in emerging hybrid, discursive-material spaces that are neither physical or virtual but a combination of the two

**Elder** established member of a community

**Emoticons** a group of characters where icons represent emotions ☺

**Flaming** aggressive tones in online communication

**Harvesting** email addresses collected from postings on the web from individuals knowingly/unknowingly

**Hybrid text** an electronic discourse in which writing reads as the spoken word (writing talking)

**IRC (internet relay chat)** is a form of real-time Internet chat or synchronous conferencing. It is mainly designed for group communication in discussion forums

**ISP (internet service provider)** is a company that provides access to the Internet. Users of the Internet must be registered with an ISP

**Lurking** practice of reading an online or email discussion without taking part in the discussion

**Macro/micro cultures** macro or large cultures of a state or society. Micro cultures are at usually at institutional or community level but the term is sometimes used to describe cultures of sub-units within an institution or community – see small cultures

**MUDS (multiuser dungeon/domain)/MOOs (MUD-object orientated)** Online virtual environments based on exchange of text and interact with other individuals

**Nettiquette** 'network etiquette', is a set of social conventions that facilitate interaction over networks, ranging from Usenet and mailing lists to blogs and forums

**Online** means being connected to the Internet and involved a variety of activities; in this context online chat/discussion – opposite of 'offline'

**Online research communities** research projects using online methods of data collection and/or communication either alone or in tandem with other online/offline methods

**Text/speech acts** the use of online text in ways that give it some of the characteristics of both written a medium of communication and a spoken one

**Third spaces** the interstices between existing social networks or communities in time and space. It is these that are colonised when people from different communities begin to establish a new (small) community for some purpose – see 'small cultures'

**Small culture** a culture constructed by a group of people coming together for some purpose. The culture is constructed out of the elements that they bring with them as individuals from the cultures of the other communities which they inhabit, as well as elements of the macro cultures around them (see Holliday 2004)

**Synchronous/real-time communications** occur at the same and same place

**Virtual ethnographies** study of Internet-based phenomena through methodologies implemented by and through the Internet (see Hine, 2005)

**Virtual reality (VR)** technology that allows a user to interact with a computer-simulated environment

# References

Addrianssens, C. and Cadman, L. (1999) 'An adaption of moderated e-maill focus groups to assess the potential of a new online (Internet) financial services offer in the UK', *Journal of the Market Research Society*, 41 (4): 417–24.

Allen, J. (2000) 'On Georg Simmel: proximity, distance and movement', in M. Crang and N. Thrift (eds), *Thinking Space*. London: Routledge. pp. 54–70.

Atkinson, P. and Hammersley, M. (1998) 'Ethnograpy and partcipant observation', in N. Denzin and Y. Lincoln (eds), *Strategies of Qualitative Inquiry*. Thousand Oaks: Sage Publications. pp. 110–26.

Atkinson, P. and Silverman, D. (1997) 'Kundera's immortality: the interview society and the invention of self', *Qualitative Inquiry*, 3 (3): 304–25.

Bacharach, S. and Lawler, E. (1980) *Power and Politics in Organisations*. San Francisco, CA: Jossey Bass.

Baez, B. (2002) 'Confidentiality in qualitative research: reflections on secrets, power and agency', *Qualitative Research*, 2 (1): 35–58.

Bahous, R., Busher, H. and Nabhani, M. (2006) 'Case studies in education in Beirut: why did one school engage students from socially disadvantaged backgrounds in learning?', European Conference on Educational Research, 13–16. September 2006, Geneva.

Bakardjieva, M. and Feenberg, A. (2000) 'Involving the virtual subject', *Ethics and Information Technology*, 2 (4): 233–40.

Bakardjieva, M. and Smith, R. (2001) 'The internet in everyday life', *New Media and Society*, 3 (1): 67–83.

Ball, S.J. (1987) *The Micro-Politics of the School*. London: Methuen.

Bampton, R. and Cowton, C.J. (2002) 'The E-interview, forum', *Qualitative Social Research*, 3 (2): Available at: http://www.qualitative-research.net/fqs/-eng.htm (accessed 10 September 2006).

Barnes, S.B. (2004) 'Issues of attribution and identification in online social research', in M.D. Johns, S.L.S. Chen and G.J. Hall (eds), *Online Social Research: Methods, Issues and Ethics*. Oxford: Peter Lang Publishing. pp. 203–22.

Barton, D. and Tusting, K. (2005) 'Introduction', in D. Barton and K. Tusting (eds), *Beyond Communities of Practice: Language, Power and Social Context*. Cambridge: Cambridge University Press. pp. 1–13

Bassett, K. and O'Riordan, K. (2002) 'Ethics of internet research: contesting the human subjects research model', *Ethics and Information Technology*, 4 (3): 233–47.

Baym, N. (1995) 'The emergence of community in computer mediated communication', in S. Jones (eds), *Cybersociety: Computer-Mediated Communication and Community*. Thousand Oaks, CA: Sage Publications. pp. 139–63.

Baym, N. (2005) 'Introduction: internet research as it isn't, is, could be, and should be', *The Information Society*, 21 (3): 229–32.

Beck, C.T. (2005) 'Benefits of participation in internet interviews: women helping women', *Qualitative Health Research*, 15 (3): 411–22.

Bennett, N. (2001) 'Power, structure and culture: an organisational view of school effectiveness and school improvement', in N. Bennett and A. Harris (eds), *School Effectiveness and School Improvement: Searching for the Elusive Partnership.* London: Continuum. pp. 75–97.

Berger, P. and Luckmann, T. (1966) *The Social Construction of Reality: A Treatise in the Sociology of Knowledge.* Garden City, NY: Doubleday.

Berger, R.M. and Patchner, M.A. (1988) 'Research Ethics', in N. Bennett, R. Glatter and R. Levacic (eds) (1994), *Improving Educational Management through Research and Consultancy.* London: Paul Chapman for the Open University.

Beaulieu, A. (2004) 'Mediating ethnography: objectivity and the making of ethnographies of the internet', *Social Epistemology*, 18 (2–3): 139–63.

Bhabha, H. (1994) *The Location of Culture.* London: Routledge.

Bishop, J. (2006) 'Increasing participation in online communities: a framework for human–computer interaction', *Computers in Human Behavior*, 23 (4): 1881–93.

Boshier, R. (1990) 'Socio-psychological factors in electronic networking', *International Journal of Life-Long Education*, 9 (1): 49–64.

Bourdieu, P. (1986) 'Forms of capital', in J.G. Richardson (ed.), *Handbook of Theory and Research for the Sociology of Education.* Santa Barbara, CA: Greenwood Press. pp. 241–58.

Bourdieu, P. (1990) *The Logic of Practice,* trans. Richard Nice. Cambridge: Polity Press.

Bourdieu, P. (1998) *Acts of Resistance.* Cambridge: Polity Press.

Bourdieu, P. and Passeron, J.-C. (1977) *Reproduction in Education: Society and Culture.* London: Sage Publications.

Bourdieu, P., Passeron, J.-C. and de St. Martin, M. (1994) *Academic Discourse.* Cambridge: Polity Press.

Bowker, N. and Tuffin, K. (2004) 'Using the online medium for discursive research about people with disabilities', *Social Science Computer Review*, 22 (2): 228–41.

British Educational Research Association (BERA) (2004) *Revised Ethical Guidelines for Educational Research.* Available at: http://www.bera.ac.uk/publications/guides. php (accessed 10 September 2006).

British Psychological Society (BPS) (2006) *Code of Ethics and Conduct.* Leicester: BPS.

British Sociological Association (BSA) (2002) *Statement of Ethical Practice for the British Sociological Association.* Durham: British Sociological Association.

Bryman, A. (2004) *Social Research Methods*, 2nd edn. Oxford: Oxford University Press.

Bruckman, A. (1992) *Identity Workshop: Emergent Social and Psychological Phenomena in Text-based Virtual Reality.* Available at: http://www.cc.gatech.edu/~asb/papers/ index.html (accessed 3 June 2008).

Bruckman, A. (2002a) 'Studying the amateur artist. A perspective on disguising data collected in human subjects research on the Internet', *Ethics and Information Technology*, 4 (3): 217–31.

Bruckman, A. (2002b) *Ethical Guidelines for Research Online.* Available at: http://www.cc.gatech.edu~asb/ethics/ (accessed 23 June 2008).

Bulmer, H. (1988) 'Some reflections on research in organisations', in A. Bryman (ed.), *Doing research in Organisations.* London: Routledge.

Burgess, R.G. (1989) 'Ethics and educational research: an introduction', in R.G. Burgess (ed.), *The Ethics of Educational Research.* London: Falmer Press.

Burkeman, O. (2008) 'The internet', *The Guardian*: 19.

Busher, H. (2001) 'Being and becoming a doctoral student: culture, literacies and self-identity', paper presented at TESOL Arabia Conference, 14–16 March.

Busher, H. (2005) 'Ethics of educational research: an agenda for discussion', Key note presentation to the Ninth *Science and Mathematics Education Conference* (SMEC 9), American University of Beirut (AUB), Lebanon, 18–19 November.

Busher, H. (2006) *Understanding Educational Leadership: People, Power and Culture*. Buckingham: Open University Press.

Capurro, R. and Pringle, C. (2002) 'Ethical issues of online communication research', *Ethics and Information Technology*, 4 (3): 189–94.

Carter, D. (2005) 'Living in virtual communities: an ethnography of human relationships in cyberspace', *Information, Communication and Society*, 8 (2): 148–67.

Cavanagh, A. (2007) *Sociology in the Age of the Internet*. Maidenhead: Open University/McGraw-Hill.

Chadwick, R. (2001) 'Ethical assessment and the human genome issues', in P. Shipley and D. Moir (eds), *Ethics in Practice in the Twenty-first Century, Proceedings of the Interdiscplinary Conference of the Society for the Furtherance of Critical Philosophy*, October 1999, Eynsham Hall, Oxon.

Chen, P. and Hinton, S.M. (1999) 'Realtime interviewing using the world wide web', *Sociological Research*, 4 (3): Available at: http://www.socresonline.org.uk/socresonline/4/3/chen/html (accessed 26 June 2006).

Chen, S., Hall, G.J. and Johns, M.D. (2004) 'Research paparazzi in cyberspace: the voices of the researched', in M.D. Johns, S. Chen and G.J. Hall (eds), *Online Social Research: Methods Issues, and Ethics*. New York: Peter Lang. pp. 157–78.

Clandinin, D.J. and Connelly, F.M. (2000) *Narrative Inquiry: Experience and Story in Qualitative Research*. San Fransciso, CA: Jossey Bass.

Clifford, J. (1997) *Routes: Travel and Translation in the Late Twentieth Century*. New York: Routledge.

Cohen, L., Manion, L. and Morrison, K. (2000) *Research Methods in Education*, 5th edn. London: Routledge Falmer.

Coleman, S. (2006) 'Email, terrorism, and the right to privacy', *Ethics and Information Technology*, 8 (4): 17–27.

Correll, S. (1995) 'The ethnography of an electronic bar: the Lesbian café', *Journal of Contemporary Ethnography*, 24 (3): 270–98.

Crotty, M. (1998) *The Foundations of Social Research. Meaning and Perspective in the Research Process*. London: Sage Publications.

Crystal, D. (2001) *Language and the Internet*. Cambridge: Cambridge University Press.

Curtis, P. (1992) 'Mudding: social phenomena in text-based virtual realities'. Available at: http://www.cpsr.org/cpsr/sociology/mud_moo/DIAC92.txt (accessed 20 June 2007).

Danet, B. (1998) 'Text as mask: gender, play and performance on the internet', *Cybersociety 2.0: Revisiting Computer-mediated Communication and Community*. Thousand Oaks, CA: Sage Publications. pp. 129–58.

Davis, B. and Brewer, J. (1997) *Electronic Discourse: Linguistic Individuals in Virtual Space*. New York: State University of New York Press.

Davis, M., Bolding, G., Hart, G., Sherr, L. and Elford, J. (2004) 'Reflecting on the experience of interviewing online: perspectives from internet and HIV study in London', *AIDS Care*, 16 (8): 944–52.

Day, G. (2006) *Community and Everyday Life*. Oxford: Routledge.

De Laine, M. (2000) *Fieldwork, Participation and Practice: Ethics and Dilemmas in Qualitative Research*. London: Sage Publications.

Delorme, D.E., Zinkhan, G.E. and French, W. (2001) 'Ethics and the internet: Issues associated with qualitative research', *Journal of Business Ethics*, 33 (4): 271–86.

Denscombe, M. (2003) *The Good Research Guide*. Maidenhead: Open University Press.

Denzin, N. (1989) *Interpretive Interactionism*. Newbury Park: CA: Sage Publications.

Denzin, N. (1999) 'Cybertalk and the method of instances', in S. Jones (ed.), *Doing Internet Research: Critical Issues and Methods for Examining the Net*. London: Sage Publications. pp. 107–25.

Denzin, N. and Lincoln, Y.S. (1994) 'Introduction: Entering the field of qualitative research', in N. Denzin and Y.S. Lincoln (eds), *Handbook of Qualitative Research*. London: Sage Publications. pp. 1–17.

Denzin, N. and Lincoln, Y.S. (2000) 'Introduction: Entering the field of qualitative research', in N. Denzin and Y.S. Lincoln (eds), *Handbook of Qualitative Research*, 2nd edn. Thousand Oakes CA: Sage Publications. pp. 10–15.

Derrida, J. (2000) *Of Hospitality*. Stanford CA: Stanford University Press.

Doherty, C. (2007) 'Compromised methods for an adaptive ethnography: researching cultural interaction in online internationalise education', paper given at the British Educational Research Association Conference, Institute of Education, University of London, 5–8 September.

Dominguez, D., Beaulieu, A., Estalella, S., Gomez, E., Schnettler, B. and Read, R. (2007) 'Virtual ethnography', *Forum: Qualitative Social Research*, 8 (3). Available at: http://www.qualitative-research.net/fqs-texte/3-07/07-3-E1-e.htm (accessed 10 December 2007).

Donarth, J.S. (2001) 'Identity and deception in the virtual community', in M.A. Smith and P. Kollock (eds.), *Communities in Cyberspace*. London: Routledge. pp. 129–59.

Duncan-Howell, J. (2007) 'Graphically mapping electronic discussions: unlocking online dynamics', British Educational Research Association Conference, Institute of Education, University of London, 5–8 September 2007.

Dominguez, D., Beaulieu, A., Estalella, S., Gomez, E., Schnettler, B. and Read, R. (2007) 'Virtual ethnography', *Forum: Qualitative Social Research*, 8 (3): Available at: http://www.qualitative-research.net/fqs-texte/3-07/07-3-E1-e.htm (accessed 10 December 2007).

Easterby-Smith, M., Thorpe, R. and Lowe, A. (1991) *Management Research: An Introduction*. London: Sage Publications.

ESRC (Economic and Social Research Council) (2005) *Research Ethics Framework*. Swindon: Economic and Social Research Council.

Eichorn, K. (2001) 'Sites unseen: ethnographic research in a textual community', *Qualitative Studies in Education*, 14 (4): 565–78.

Eisenhart, M. (2001) 'Educational ethnography past, present and future. Ideas to think with', *Educational Researcher*, 30 (8): 16–27.

Elgesem, D. (2002) 'What is special about the ethical issues in online research?', *Ethics and Information Technology*, 4 (1): 195–203.

Ess, C. and the Association of Internet Researchers (AoIR) (2002) 'Ethical decision-making and internet research'. Available at: http://www.aoir.org/reports/ethics.pdf (accessed 10 April 2006).

Ess, C. (2004) 'Epilogue: are we there yet? Emerging ethical guidelines for online research', in M.D. Johns, S.S. Chen and G.J. Hall (eds), *Online Social Research: Methods, Issues and Ethics*. New York: Peter Lang. pp. 253–64.

Evans, K.F. (2004) *Maintaining Community in the Information Age: The Importance of Trust, Place and Situated Knowledge*. Palgrave Macmillan.

Eysenbach, G. and Till, J.E. (2001) 'Ethical issues in qualitative research on internet communities', *British Medical Journal*, 10; 323 (7321): 1103–5.

Flick, U. (2002) *An Introduction to Qualitative Research*, 2nd edn. London: Sage Publications.

Fontana, A. and Frey, J.H. (2003) 'The interview: from structured questions to negotiated text', in N.K. Denzin and Y.S. Lincoln (eds), *Collecting and Interpreting Qualitative Materials*. London: Sage Publications. pp. 149–60.

Foster, P. (2006) 'Observational research', in R. Sapsford and V. Jupp (eds), *Data Collection and Analysis*. London: Sage Open University, pp. 57–93.

Foucault, M. (1975) *Birth of the Clinic: An Archaeology of Medical Perception*, trans. A.M. Sheridan. New York: Vintage/Random House.

Foucault, M. (1976) 'Truth and Power', in C. Gordon (ed.) (1980) *Power/Knowledge: Selected Interviews and other Writings by Michel Foucault, 1972–1977*. New York: Pantheon Books, pp. 109–33.

Foucault, M. (1977) *Discipline and Punish: The Birth of the Prison*, trans. A. Sheridan Harmondsworth: Penguin.

Foucault, M. (1994) 'The subject and power', in J.D Faubion (ed.), *Essential Works of Foucault, 1954–1984, volume 3, Power*. London: Penguin.

Fox, N. and Roberts, C. (1999) 'GPs in cyberspace: the sociology of a virtual community', *The Sociological Review*, 47 (4): 643–71.

Fox, J., Murray, C. and Warm, A. (2003) 'Conducting research using web-based questionnaires: practical, methodological and ethical considerations', *International Journal of Social Research Methodology*, 6 (2): 167–80.

French, J. and Raven, B. (1968) 'The bases of social power', in D. Cartwright and A. Zander (eds), *Group Dynamics, Research and Theory*. London: Tavistock Press. pp. 351–61.

Gaiser, T. (1997) 'Conducting on-line focus groups: a methodological discussion', *Social Science Computer Review*, 15 (2): 135–44.

Gatson, S.N. and Zweerink, A. (2004) 'Ethnography online: "Natives" practising and inscribing community', *Qualitative Research*, 4 (2): 179–200.

Geertz, C. (1973) *The Interpretation of Cultures*. New York: Basic Books.

Giddens, A. (1984) *The Constitution of Society*. Berkley, CA: University of California.

Giddens, A. (1990) *The Consequences of Modernity*. Stanford, CA: Stanford University Press.

Giddens, A. (1991) *Modernity and Self-identity*. Cambridge: Polity Press.

Gilbert, P.K. and Dabbagh, N. (2005) 'How to structure online discussions for meaningful discourse: a case study', *British Journal of Educational Technology*, 36 (1): 5–18.

Giese, M. (1998) 'Self without body: textual self-representation in an electronic community', *First Monday*, 3 (4): Available at: http://www.firstmonday.dk/issues3_4/giese/index.html (accessed 6 January 2008).

Goffman, E. (1959) *The Presentation of Self in Everyday Life*. New York: Doubleday.

Goodfellow, R. (2007) 'The impact of emerging web 2.0 Internet practices on future developments in teaching and learning', paper presented at Learning Futures Conference, University of Leicester, 9–10 January.

Gotved, S. (2006) 'Time and space in cyber social reality', *New Media and Society*, 8 (3): 467–86.

Hall, G.J., Frederick, D. and Johns, M.D. (2004) '"Need help ASAP!!!": A feminist communitarian approach to online research ethics', in M.D. Johns, S.L.S. Chen and G.J. Hall (eds), *Online Social Research: Methods, Issues and Ethics*. Oxford: Peter Lang Publishing. pp. 239–52.

Hammersley, M. (1998) *Reading Ethnographic Research: An Ethical Guide*. London: Longman.

Hammersley, M. (2006) 'Ethnography: problems and prospects', *Ethnography and Education,* 1 (1): 3–14.

Hammersley, M. and Treseder, P. (2007) 'Identity as an analytic problem: who's who in 'pro-ana' websites?', *Qualitative Research*, 7 (3): 283–300.

Hardy, C. (1985) 'The Nature of Unobtrusive Power', *Journal of Management Studies,* 22 (4): 384–99.

Hardey, M. (2002) 'Life beyond the screen: embodiment and identity through the internet', *The Sociological Review*, 50 (4): 570–85.

Hardey, M. (2004) 'Digital life stories: Auto/biography in the information age', *Auto/Biography,* 12: 183–200.

Henson, A. Koivu-Rybicki, V., Madigan, D. and Muchmore, J.A. (2000) 'Researching teaching through collaborative inquiry with outside researchers', in A. Cole, A. and J.G. Knowles (eds), *Researching Teaching: Exploring Teacher Development Through Reflexive Inquiry.* Boston, MA: Allwyn & Bacon. pp. 186–97.

Hessler, R.M., Downing, J., Beltz, C., Pellicio, A., Powell, M., Vale, W. (2003) 'Qualitative research on adloscent risk using email: a methodological assessment', *Qualitative Sociology* 26 (1): 111–24.

Hine, C. (2000) *Virtual Ethnography*. London: Sage Publications.

Hine, C. (2004) 'Social Research methods and the Internet: a thematic view', *Sociological Research Online*, 9 (2): Available at: http://www.socresonline.org.uk/9/2/hine.html (accessed 20 May 2008).

Hine, C. (2005) *Virtual Methods: Issues in Social Research on the Internet.* Oxford: Berg.

Hinton-Smith, T. (2006) 'Lone parents as higher education students: a qualitative email study', paper presented at the European Society for Research on the Education of Adults Access, Learning Careers and Identities Network Conference, 7–9 December.

Hofstede, G. (1991) *Cultures and Organizations: Software of the Mind*. London: McGraw-Hill.

Hodgson, S. (2004) 'Cutting through the silence, a sociological construction of self-injury', *Sociological Inquiry*, 74 (2): 162–79.

Hodkinson, P. (2004) 'Research as a form of work: expertise, community and methodological objectivity', *British Educational Research Journal,* 30 (1): 9–26.

Holliday, A. (1994) *Appropriate Methodology and Social Context*. Cambridge: Cambridge University Press.

Holliday, A. (2004) *Intercultural Communication: An Advanced Resource Book*. London: Routledge.

Hookway, N. (2008) '"Entering the blogopshere": some strategies for using blogs in social research', *Qualitative Research* 8 (1): 91–113.

Illingworth, N. (2001) 'The internet matters: exploring the use of the internet as a research tool, Sociological Research Online, 6 (2): Available at: http://www.socres online.org.uk/6/2/illingworth.html (accessed 14 September 2004).

Illingworth, N. (2006) 'Content, context, reflexivity and the qualitative research encounter: telling stories in the virtual realm', *Sociological Research Online,* 11 (1): Available at: http://www.socresonline.org.uk/11/1/illingworth.html, (accessed 10 December 2007).

Isabella, S. (2007) 'Ethnography of online role-playing games: the role of virtual and real contest in the construction of the field', *Forum Qualitative Research* 8 (3): Art. 36. Available at: http://www.qualitative-research.net/fqs-texte/3-07/07-3-36-e.htm (accessed 10 December 2007).

Jacobson, D. (1999) 'Doing research in cyberspace', *Field Methods,* 11 (2): 127–45.

James, N.R. (2003) 'Teacher professionalism, teacher identity: how do I see myself?', unpublished doctorate of education thesis, University of Leicester, School of Education, July 2003.

James, N. (2007) 'The use of email interviewing as a qualitative method of inquiry in educational research', *British Educational Research Journal,* 33 (6): 963–76.

James, N. and Busher, H. (2006) 'Credibility, authenticity and voice: dilemmas in web-based interviewing', *Qualitative Research Journal,* 6 (3): 403–20.

James, N. and Busher, H. (2007) 'Ethical issues in online educational research: protecting privacy, establishing authenticity in email interviewing', *International Journal of Research and Method in Education,* 30 (1): 101–13.

Janelle, D.G. and Hodges, D.C. (2000) *Information, Place and Cyberspace.* New York: Springer.

Jankowski N.W. and van Selm, M. (2005) 'Epilogue: methodological concerns and innovations in internet research', in C. Hine (ed.), *Virtual Methods: Issues in Social Research on the Internet.* Oxford: Berg. pp. 21–34.

Johns, M.D. Chen S.L.S. and Hall G.J. (eds) (2004) *Online Social Research: Methods, Issues and Ethics.* Oxford: Peter Lang Publishing.

Joinson, A.N. (2001) 'Self-disclosure in computer-mediated communication: the role of self-awareness and visual anonymity', *European Journal of Social Psychology,* 31 (2): 177–92.

Joinson, A.N. (2005) 'Internet behaviour and the design of virtual methods', in C. Hine, (ed.), *Virtual Methods: Issues in Social Research on the Internet.* Oxford: Berg. pp. 21–34.

Jones, S. (1999) *Doing Internet Research: Critical issues and Methods for Examining the Net.* Thousand Oaks: CA: Sage Publications.

Jones, S. (2004) 'Introduction: ethics and internet studies', in M.D. Johns, S.L.S. Chen and G.J. Hall (eds), *Online Social Research: Methods, Issues and Ethics.* Oxford: Peter Lang Publishing. pp. 179–86.

Jordan, T. (1999) 'Cyberpower and the meaning of online activism', *Cybersociology,* 1 (5): Available at: http://www.cybersociology.com/files/5_timjordan_ cyberpower. html (accessed 30 June 2008).

Kanayama, T. (2003) 'Ethnographic research on the experience of Japanese elderly people online', *New Media and Society,* 5 (2): 267–88.

Kearney, C. (2003) *The Monkey's Mask: Identity, Memory, Narrative and Voice.* Stoke-on-Trent: Trentham Books.

Kendall, L. (1999) 'Recontextualisng "cyberspace" methodological considerations for online research', in S. Jones (ed.), *Doing Internet Research Critical Issues and Methods for Examining the Net.* London: Sage Publications. pp. 57–75.

Kennedy, H. (2006) 'Beyond anonymity, or future directions of internet identity research', *New Media and Society,* 8 (6): 859–76.

Kibby, M.D. (2005) 'Email forwardables folklore in the age of the internet', *New Media and Society,* 7 (6): 770–90.

Kim, A.J. (2000) *Community Building on the Web: Secret Strategies for Successful Online Communities.* Berkeley, CA: Peachpit Press.

King, S.A. (1996) 'Researching internet communities: proposed ethical guidelines for reporting results', *The Information Society,* 12 (2): 119–27.

Kivits, J. (2005) 'Online interviewing and the research relationship', in C. Hine (ed.), *Virtual Methods: Issues in Social Research on the Internet.* Oxford: Berg. pp. 35–50.

Klester, S. (1994) 'Working together apart', *Cause/Effect,* 17 (3): 8–12.

Knight, P.T. and Saunders, M. (1999) 'Understanding teachers' professional cultures through interview: a constructivist approach', *Evaluation and Research in Education,* 13 (3): 144–56.

Knoebel, M. (2005) 'Rants, ratings and representation: ethical issues in researching online social practices', in K. Sheehy, M. Nind, J. Rix and K. Simmons (eds), *Ethics and Research in Inclusive Education. Values into Practice.* London: RoutledgeFalmer/The Open University. pp. 150–67.

Kolko, B. and Reid, E. (1998) 'Dissolution and fragmentation: problems in online communities', in S. Jones (ed.), *Cybersociety 2.0: Revisiting Computer-mediated Communication and Community.* Thousand Oaks, CA: Sage Publications. pp. 212–29.

Kraut, R., Olson, J., Banaji, M., Bruckman, A., Cohen, J. and Couper, M. (2004) 'Psychological research online: report of the board of scientific affairs' advisory group on the conduct of research on the internet', *American Psychologist,* 59 (2): 105–17.

Kress, G. (2000) 'Design and transformation: new theories of meaning', in B. Cope and M. Kalantis (eds), *Multi-literacies: Literacy, Learning and the Design of Social Futures.* London: Routledge.

Lave, J. and Wenger, E. (1991) *Situated Learning: Legitimate Peripheral Participation* Cambridge: Cambridge University Press.

Lee, H. (2006) 'Privacy, publicity and accountability of self-presentation in an online discussion group', *Sociological Inquiry,* 76 (1): 1–22.

Lebesco, K. (2004) 'Managing visibility, intimacy, and focus in online critical ethnography', in M.D. Johns, S.L.S. Chen, and G.J. Hall (eds), *Online Social Research: Methods, Issues and Ethics.* Oxford: Peter Lang Publishing. pp. 63–80.

Lefebvre, H. (1974) *The Production of Space.* Malden, MA: Blackwell.

Levinson, B.A., Foley, D.E., and Holland, D.C (eds) (1996) *The Cultural Production of the Educated Person: Critical Ethnographies of Schooling and Local Practice.* New York: State University of New York Press.

Lenski, G. (1986) 'Power and privilege', in S. Lukes (ed.), *Power.* Oxford: Blackwell. pp. 243–252.

Lincoln, Y.S. and Guba, E.G. (1985) *Naturalistic Inquiry.* Beverly Hills: CA: Sage Publications.

Lincoln, Y.S. and Guba, E.G. (2000) 'Paradigmatic controversies, contradictions, and emerging confluences', in N.K. Denzin and Y.S. Lincoln (eds), *Handbook of Qualitative Research,* 2nd edn. Thousand Oaks CA: Sage Publications. pp. 163–88.

Lukes, S. (1974) *Power: A Radical View.* New York: The Macmillan Press.

Ma, R. (1996) 'Computer-mediated conversations as a new dimension of intercultural communication between East Asian and North American college students', in S. Herring (ed.), *Computer-Mediated Communication: Linguistic, Social and Cross Cultural Perspectives.* Amsterdam: John Benjamins Publishing. pp. 173–86.

McKee, H. and Porter. J.E. 'The ethics of digital writing research: a rhetorical approach', *College Composition and Communication,* 59 (4): 711–49.

Maclure, M. (1995) 'Postmodernism: a postscript', *Educational Action Research,* 3 (1): 105–6.

Madge, C. (2006) 'Online research ethics'. Available at: http://www.geog.le.ac.uk/orm/onlineresearchethics.htm (accessed 10 December 2007).

Madge, C. (2007) 'Developing a geographers' agenda for online research ethics', *Progress in Human Geography,* 31 (5): 654–74.

Madge, C. and O'Connor, H. (2005) 'Mothers in the making? Exploring notions of liminality in hybrid cyberspace', Transactions of the Institute of British Geographers, 3 (1): 83–97.

Madge, C., O'Connor, H., Wellens, J., Hookey, T. and Shaw, R. (2006) Exploring online research methods in a virtual training environment. Available at: http://www.geog.le.ac.uk/orm (accessed on 1 May 2007).

Mann, C. and Stewart, F. (2000) *Internet Communication and Qualitative Research: A Handbook for Researching Online.* London: Sage Publications.

Mariampolski, H. (1999) 'The power of ethnography', *Journal of Market Research,* 41 (1): 75–86.

Markham, A.M. (1998) *Life Online: Researching Real Experience in Virtual Space.* Walnut Creek CA: AltaMira Press.

Markham, A. (2004a) 'The internet as research context', in C. Seale G. Gobo, J.F. Gubrium and D. Silverman (eds), *Qualitative Research Practice.* London: Sage Publications. pp. 328–44.

Markham, A.N. (2004b) 'Representation in online ethnography', in M.D. Johns, S.L.S. Chen and G.J. Hall (eds), *Online Social Research: Methods, Issues and Ethics.* Oxford: Peter Lang Publishing. pp. 141–57.

Massey, D. (1994) *Space, Place and Gender.* Cambridge: Polity Press.

Masson, J. (2005) 'Researching children's perspectives: legal issues', in K. Sheehly, M. Nind, J. Rix and K. Simmons (eds), *Ethics and Research in Inclusive Education: Values into Practice.* London: RoutledgeFalmer. pp. 231–42.

Matthews, S. (2006) 'On-line professionals', *Ethics and Information Technology,* 8 (2): 61–71.

Mathews, J. and Cramer, E.P. (2008) 'Using technology to enhance qualitative research with hidden populations', *The Qualitative Report,* 13 (2): 301–15. Available at http://www.nova.edu.ssss/QR/Qr13-2/mathews.pdf (accessed 27 June 2008)

Maynard, M. (1994) 'Methods, practice and epistemology: the debate about feminism and research', in M. Maynard and J. Purvis (eds), *Researching Women's Lives from a Feminist Perspective.* London: Taylor and Francis, pp. 10–26.

Miller, D. and Slater, D. (2000) *The Internet: An Ethnographic Approach.* Oxford: Berg.

Mitra, A. and Cohen, E. (1999) 'Analysing the web: directions and challenges', in S. Jones (eds), *Doing Internet Research: Critical Issues and Methods for Examining the Net.* London: Sage Publications. pp. 179–242.

Mittendorf, K., Geijsel, F., Hoeve, A., Laat, M.D. and Niewenhuis, L. (2005) 'Communities of practice as stimulating forces for collective learning', *Journal of Workplace Learning,* 18 (5): 298–312.

Mulkay, M., Potter, J. and Yearley, S. (1983) 'Why an analysis of scientific discourse is needed', in K.D. Knorr-Cetina and M. Mulkay (eds) *Science Observed: Perspectives on the Social Studies of Science,* London: Sage Publications, pp. 171–204.

Murray, C. and Sixsmith, J. (1998) 'Email: a qualitative research medium for interviewing?', *International Journal of Social Research Methodology,* 1 (2): 103–21.

National Committees for Research Ethics in Norway (NESH) (2006) Guidelines for Research Ethics in the Social Sciences, Law and the Humanities. Available at: http://www.etikkom.no/English/NESH/guidelines (accessed 20 May 2008).

National Committee for Research Ethics in the Social sciences and the Humanities (NESH) in Norway (2003) *Research Ethics Guidelines for Internet Research* English translation approved by NESH 3 December 2003. Available at: http://www.etikkom.no/English/NESH/guidelines (accessed 20 May 2008).

Oakley, A. (1981) 'Interviewing women: a contradiction in terms', in H. Roberts (ed.), *Doing Feminist Research.* London: Routledge. pp. 30–61.

O'Connor, H. and Madge, C. (2001) 'Cybermothers: online synchronous interviewing using conferencing software', *Sociological Research Online,* 5 (4): Available at: http://www.socresonline.org.uk/5/4/o'connor.html (accessed 10 September 2006.)

O'Connor, H. and Madge, C. (2003) 'Focus groups in cyberspace': using the internet for qualitative research', *Qualitative Market Research: An International Journal,* 6 (2): 133–43.

Orgad, S. (2005) 'From online to offline and back: moving from online to offline relationships with research participants', in C. Hines (ed.), *Virtual Methods: Issues in Social Research on the Internet.* Oxford: Berg. pp. 51–66.

Orgad, S. (2006) 'The cultural dimensions of online communication: a study of breast cancer patients' internet spaces', *New Media and Society,* 8 (6): 877–99.

Paccagnella, L. (1997) 'Getting the seats of your pants dirty: strategies for ethnographic research on virtual communities', *Journal of Computer-Mediated Communication,* 3 (1): Available at: http://www.ascusc.org/jcmc/vol3/issue1/paccagnella.html.

Parsons, T. (1986) 'Power and the social system', in S. Lukes (ed.), *Power.* Oxford: Blackwell. pp. 286–99.

Pittinger, D. (2003) 'Internet research: an opportunity to revisit classic ethical problems in behavioural research', *Ethics and Behaviour,* 13 (1): 45–60.

Phippen, A. (2007) 'How virtual are virtual methods?', *Methodological Innovations Online,* 2 (1): Available at: http://erdt.plymouth.ac.uk/mionline/publichtml/viewarticle.php? id=43 (accessed 23 June 2008).

Postmes, T., Spears, R. and Lea, M. (1998) 'Breaching or building social boundaries? SIDE-effect of computer-mediated communication', *Communications Research*, 25 (6): 689–715.

Popkewitz and L. Fendler (eds), *Critical Theories in Education*. London: Routledge. pp. 45–65.

Preece, J. (2004) 'Etiquette and trust drive online communities of practice', *Journal of Universal Computer Science*, 10 (3): 294–302.

Psathas, G. (1995) *Conversation Analysis*. Thousand Oaks CA: Sage Publications.

Reed, K. (2004) 'You've got mail ...', *AUTLOOK*, 231: 14.

Rheingold, H. (1994) *The Virtual Community: Finding Connection in a Computerised World*. London: Secker and Warburg.

Richardson, L. (1997) *Fields of Play: Constructing an Academic Life*. New Brunswick, NJ: Rutgers University Press.

Robbins, S.P. (2003) *Organisational Behaviour*, 10th edn. Upper Saddle River, NJ: Prentice Hall.

Robson, K. and Robson, M. (2002) 'Your place or mine? Ethics, the researcher and the Internet', in T. Welland and L. Pugsley (eds), *Ethical Dilemmas in Qualitative Research*. London: Ashgate. pp. 94–107.

Rodgers, J. (2004) 'Doreen Massey: space, relations' communications', *Information, Communication and Society*, 7 (2): 273–91.

Ruhleder, K. (2000) 'The virtual ethnographer: fieldwork in distributed electronic environments', *Field Methods*, 12 (1): 3–17.

Russell, T. and Bullock, S. (1999) 'Discovering our professional knowledge as teachers: critical dialogues about learning from experience', in J. Loughran (ed.), *Researching Methodologies and Practices for Understanding Pedagogy*. NewYork: The Falmer Press, pp, 132–51.

Rutter, J. and Smith, G.W.H. (2005) 'Ethnographic presence in a nebulous setting', in C. Hine (ed.), *Virtual Methods: Issues in Social Research on the Internet*. Oxford: Berg. pp. 81–92.

Rybas, N. and Gajjala, R. (2007) 'Developing cyberethnographic research methods for understanding digitally mediated identities', *Forum: Qualitative Social Research*, 8 (3), Art. 35. Available at: http://www.qualitative-research.net/fqs-texte/3-07/07-3-35-e.htm (accessed 10 December 2007).

Sade-Beck, L. (2004) Internet ethnography: Online and offline, *International Journal of Qualitative Methods*, 3 (2): 1–14. Available at: http://www.ualberta.ca/~iiqm/backissues/3_2/pdf/sadebeck.pdf (accessed on 3 May 2005).

Sammons, P. (1989) 'Ethical issues and statistical work', in R.G. Burgess (ed.), *The Ethics of Educational Research*. London: Falmer Press, pp. 31–59.

Sanders, T. (2005) 'Researching the online sex work community', in C. Hine (ed.), *Virtual Methods: Issues in Social Research on the Internet*. Oxford: Berg. pp. 67–80.

Schneider, S.J., Kerwin, J., Frechtling, J. and Vivari, B.J. (2002) 'Characteristics of the discussion in online and face-to-face focus groups', *Social Science Computer Review*, 20 (1): 31–42.

Schwandt, T. (2000) 'Three epistemological stances in qualitative inquiry: interpretivism, hermeuntics and social constructionism', in N.K. Denzin and Y.S. Lincoln (eds), *Handbook of Qualitative Research*, 2nd edn. Thousand Oaks, CA: Sage Publications. pp. 189–207.

Seymour, W. (2001) 'In the flesh or online: exploring qualitative research methodologies', *Qualitative Research*, 1 (2): 147–68.

Selwyn, N. and Robson, K. (1998). 'Using email as a research tool', *Social Research Update*, Department of Sociology, University of Surrey.

Sharf, B.F (1999) 'Beyond Netiquette: the ethics of doing naturalistic research on the internet', in S. Jones (ed.), *Doing Internet Research: Critical Issues and Methods for Examining the Net*. Thousand Oaks, CA: Sage Publications. pp. 243–56.

Sikes, P. (2006) 'On dodgy ground? problematics and ethics in educational research', *International Journal of Research and Method in Education*, 29 (1): 105–17.

Silverman, D. (1999) *Doing Qualitative Research: A Practical Handbook*. London: Sage Publications.

Slater, D. (2002) 'Making things real. Ethics and order on the Internet', *Theory, Culture and Society*, 19 (5/6): 227–45.

Smith, A.D. (2001) 'Problems of conflict management in virtual communities', in M.A. Smith and P. Kollock (eds), *Communities in Cyberspace*. London: Routledge. pp. 134–63.

Smith, C. (1997) 'Casting the net: surveying an internet population', *Journal of Computer Mediated Communication*, 3 (1): Available at: http://jcmc.huji.ac.il/vol3/issue1/smith.html (accessed 23 June 2007).

Spears, R. and Lea, M. (1994) 'Panacea or panopticon? The hidden power in computer mediated communication', *Communications Research*, 21 (4): 427–59.

Sproull, L. and Kiesler, S. (1986) 'Reducing social context cues: electronic mail in organizational communication', *Management Science*, 32 (11): 1492–512.

Sproull, L. and Kiesler, S. (1991) *Connections: New Ways of Working in the Networked Organization*. Cambridge, MA: MIT Press.

Stewart, K. and Williams, M. (2005) 'Researching online populations: the use of online focus groups for social research', *Qualitative Research*, 5 (4): 395–416.

Stones, R. (1996) *Sociological Reasoning: Towards a Post-modern Sociology*. Houndmills: Macmillan Press.

Stone, A. (1996) *The War of Desire and Technology at the Close of the Mechanical Age*. Cambridge, MA: MIT Press.

Synodinos, N.E. and Brennan, J.M. (1988) 'Computer interactive interviewing in survey research', *Psychology and Marketing*, 5 (2): 117–37.

Tanis, M. and Postmes, T. (2005) 'Two faces of anonymity: paradoxical effects of cues to identity in CMC', *Computers in Human Behaviour*, 23 (2): 955–70.

Teli, M., Francesco, P. and Hakken, D. (2007) 'The internet as a library-of-people: for cyberethnography of online groups', *Forum: Qualitative Social Research*, 8 (3): Art. 33. Available at: http://www.qualitative-research.net/fqs-texte/3-07/07-3-33-e.htm (accessed 10 December 2007).

Thach, L. (1995) 'The use of electronic mail to conduct survey research', *Educational Technology*, March–April, pp. 27–31.

Thurlow, C., Lengel, L. and Tomic, A. (2004) *Computer Mediated Communication: Social Interaction and the Internet*. London: Sage Publications.

Torres, C.A. (1999) 'Critiical theory and political sociology of education: arguments', in T.S. Popkewitz and L. Fendler (eds), *Critical Theories in Education*. London: Routledge. pp. 45–65.

Trompenaars, F. and Woolliams, P. (2003) 'A new framework for managing change across cultures', *Journal of Change Management*, 3 (4): 361–74.

Turkle, S. (1995) *Life on the Screen, Identity in the Age of the Internet.* London: Phoenix/Orion.

Usher, R. (2000) 'Deconstructive happening, ethical moment', in H. Simons and R. Usher (eds), *Situated Ethics in Educational Research.* London: RoutledgeFalmer, pp. 162–85.

Van Mannen, J. (1988) *Tales of the Field: On Writing Ethnography.* Chicago, IL: University of Chicago Press.

Walford, G. (2006) 'Research ethical guidelines and anonymity', *International Journal of Research and Method in Education*, 28 (1): 83–93.

Walker, K. (2000) 'It's difficult to hide it: the presentation of self on internet home pages', *Qualitative Sociology*, 23 (1): 99–119.

Walstrom, M.K. (2004) 'Seeing and Sensing online interaction: an interpretive interactionist approach to USERNET support group research', in M.D. Johns, S.L.S. Chen and G.J. Hall (eds), *Online Social Research: Methods, Issues and Ethics.* Oxford: Peter Lang Publishing. pp. 81–100.

Walther, J.B. (2002) 'Research ethics in internet-enabled research: human subects issues and methodological myopia', *Ethics and Information Technology*, 4 (3): 205–16.

Ward, K.J. (1999) 'The Cyber-Ethnographic (Re)Construction of Two Feminist Online Communities', *Sociological Research Online*, 4 (1): Available at: http://www.socresonline.org.uk/socresonline/4/1/ward.html (accessed 10th December, 2007).

Waskul, D. and Douglass, M. (1996) 'Considering the electronic participant: some polemical observations on the ethics of on-line research', *The Information Society*, 12 (2): 129–39.

Waskul, D. and Douglass, M. (1997) 'Cyberself: the emergence of self in on-line chat', *Information Society*, 13 (4): 375–98.

Weber, M. (1947) *The Theory of Social and Economic Organisations*, trans. A.M. Henderson and H. Talcott Parsons. Glencoe, IL: Free Press.

Wenger, E. (1998) *Communities of Practice: Learning, Meaning, and Identity.* New York: Cambridge University Press.

White, M. (2002) 'Representations or people?', *Ethics and Information Technology*, 4 (3): 249–66.

Whitty, M.T. (2002) 'Liar, liar! An examination of how open, supportive and honest people are in chat rooms', *Computers in Human Behaviour*, 18 (4): 343–52.

Williams, M. (2003) 'Virtually criminal: deviance and harm within online environments', unpublished PhD thesis, University of Wales: Cardiff.

Williams, J.P. (2006) 'Authentic identities: straightedge subculture, music and the internet', *Journal of Contemporary Ethnography*, 35 (2): 173–200.

Williams, M. and Robson, K. (2004) 'Reengineering focus group methodology for the online environment', in M.D. Johns, S.L.S. Chen, and G.J. Hall (eds), *Online Social Research: Methods, Issues and Ethics.* Oxford: Peter Lang Publishing. pp. 25–46.

Wilson, S.M. and Peterson, L.C. (2002) 'The anthropology of online communities', *Annual Review of Anthropology*, 31 (1): 449–67.

Wittel, A. (2000) 'Ethnography on the move: from field to Net to Internet', *Forum: Qualitative Social Research,* 1 (1): Available at: http://www.qualitative-research.net/fqs-exte/1-00/1-00wittel-e.htm (accessed 10 December 2007).

Wolfreys, J. (1998) *Deconstruction-Derrida.* London: Macmillan Press.

Wood, C. (2005) 'Data protection issues in educational research', in K. Sheehly, M. Nind, J. Rix and K. Simmons (eds), *Ethics and Research in Inclusive Education: Values into Practice.* London: RoutledgeFalmer. pp. 242–50.

Wyn, E. and Katz, J. (1997) 'Hyperbole over cyberspace: self presentation and social boundaries in internet home pages and discourse', *The Information Society*, 13 (4): 297–327.

Xie, B. (2007) 'Using the internet for offline relationship formation', *Social Science Computer Review*, 25 (3): 396–404.

Zhao, S. (2006) 'The internet and the transformation of the reality of everyday life: towards a new analytic stance in sociology', *Sociological Inquiry*, 76 (4): 458–74.

# Author Index

ESRC (Economic and Social Research Council) 57, 58, 59, 60, 65, 115, 116, 117

Ess, C. 56, 61, 62, 63, 66, 87, 116, 126, 131

Estalella, S. 6, 33, 40

Evans, K.F. 83, 85, 87, 99, 128

Eysenbach, G. 68

Feenberg, A. 52, 63, 68, 86, 88, 92, 123

Flick, U. 12

Foley, D.E. 99

Fontana, A. 12

Foster, P. 10

Foucault, M. 12, 45, 53, 84, 86, 89, 91

Fox, J. 119, 122, 123

Fox, N. 34, 62, 81, 111

Francesco, P. 11, 13, 35

Frechtling, J. 24, 27

Frederick, D. 64, 65

French, J. 85

French, W. 60

Frey, J.H. 12

Gaiser, T. 77

Gajjala, R. 10, 35, 36

Gatson, S.N. 22, 63, 75, 78

Geertz, C. 28

Geijsel, F. 44

Giddens, A. 9, 32, 44, 46, 47, 61, 74, 87, 89, 95, 98

Giese, M. 24, 78

Gilbert, P.K. 132, 134

Goffman, E. 24, 74, 111

Gomez, E. 6, 33, 40

Goodfellow, R. 5

Gotved, S. 42, 43, 45

Gronn, P. 92

Guba, E.G. 9, 21, 136

Hakken, D. 11, 13, 35

Hall, G.J. 56, 64, 65, 124, 125, 131

Hammersley, M. 6, 7, 12, 17, 31, 69, 77

Hardey, M. 49, 75, 79

Hardy, C. 87

Hart, G. 110, 111

Henson, A. 25, 49

Hessler, R.M. 86, 88, 122, 123

Hine, C. 6, 20, 21, 28, 30, 32, 33, 34, 35, 36, 37, 40, 48, 54, 77, 78, 79, 82, 87, 106, 111, 112, 133, 136, 138, 139

Hinton-Smith, T. 12

Hinton, S.M. 54

Hodges, D.C. 87, 128

Hodgson, S. 48, 64

Hodkinson, P. 102

Hoeve, A. 44

Hofstede, G. 94

Holland, D.C. 99

Holliday, A. 97, 99, 102, 103

Hookway, N. 60, 95, 138

Hooley, T. 6

Illingworth, N. 7, 10, 11, 13, 17, 39, 54, 79, 130, 132

Isabella, S. 21

Jacobson, D. 67

James, N. 17, 24, 25, 26, 28, 29, 30, 32, 36, 37, 48, 49, 50, 52, 54, 66, 67, 76, 77, 78, 79, 80, 81, 82, 90, 92, 108, 111, 113, 129

Janelle, D.G. 87, 128

Jankowski N.W. 6, 89, 129

Johns, M.D. 56, 64, 65, 124, 125, 131

Joinson, A.N. 19, 20, 21, 22, 24, 26, 53, 83, 88, 100, 136

Jones, S. 6, 17, 69, 78, 111

Jordan, T. 91

Kanayama, T. 22, 24, 76, 119

Katz, J. 17

Kearney, C. 88, 89

Kendall, L. 35, 73, 77, 78, 80, 81

Kennedy, H. 71, 73

Kerwin, J. 24, 27

Kibby, M.D. 106, 107

Kiesler, S. 20, 32, 52, 53

Kim, A.J. 91

King, S.A. 63

Kivits, J. 24, 48, 109

Knight, P.T. 53

Knoebel, M. 57

Koivu-Rybicki, V. 25, 49

Kolko, B. 73

Kraut, R. 122

Kress, G. 89, 136

Laat, M.D. 44

Lave, J. 91, 99

Lawler, E. 85

Lea, M. 20, 21

Lebesco, K. 37, 53, 81, 92

Lee, H. 42, 49, 53, 54, 67, 68, 72, 74, 79, 80, 82, 88, 89, 100, 105, 123

Lefebvre, H. 42

Lengel, L. 109

Lenski, G. 87

Levinson, B.A. 99

Lincoln, Y.S. 9, 21, 29, 136

Lowe, A. 92

Luckmann, T. 45, 74, 89

Lukes, S. 84

Ma, R. 90
Maclure, M. 9
Madge, C. 6, 13, 26, 27, 64, 78, 81, 86, 87,
   89, 115, 123, 135
Madigan, D. 25, 49
Manion, L. 57, 58, 60, 119
Mann, C. 6, 11, 17, 21, 28, 33, 39, 48, 52,
   53, 59, 75, 77, 79, 80, 90, 106, 107, 111,
   115, 121, 131, 136
Mariampolski, H. 31
Markham, A.N. 23, 24, 28, 33, 34, 36, 38, 39,
   52, 77, 108, 109, 131
Massey, D. 44, 45, 91
Masson, J. 66
Mathews, J. 121, 125, 126, 132, 138
Matthews, S. 77, 104
Maynard, M. 7
McKee, H. 121, 124
Miller, D. 35
Mitra, A. 112
Mittendorf, K. 44
Morrison, K. 57, 58, 60, 119
Muchmore, J.A. 25, 49
Mulkay, M. 112
Murray, C. 48, 106, 119, 122, 123

Nabhani, M. 89
National Committee for Research Ethics in
   the Social sciences and the Humanities
   (NESH) 61, 63, 116, 117, 118
Niewenhuis, L. 44

O'Connor, H. 6, 13, 26, 27, 78, 81, 87
O'Riordan, K. 44, 121, 126
Oakley, A. 12, 52, 91, 92
Olson, J. 122
Orgad, S. 21, 36, 37, 38, 39, 40, 133

Paccagnella, L. 19, 21, 81, 88
Parsons, T. 84
Passeron, J.-C. 89, 99
Patchner, M.A. 69
Pellicio, A. 86, 88, 122, 123
Peterson, L.C. 77
Phippen, A. 95, 138
Pringle, C. 9, 62, 69, 118
Pittinger, D. 122
Porter. J.E. 121, 124
Postmes, T. 20
Potter, J. 112
Powell, M. 86, 88, 122, 123
Preece, J. 19
Psathas, G. 111, 112

Raven, B. 85
Read, R. 6, 33, 40

Reed, K. 87, 110
Reid, E. 63, 73
Rheingold, H. 20, 26, 136
Richardson, L. 7
Robbins, S.P. 99
Roberts, C. 34, 62, 81, 111
Robson, K. viii, 47, 61, 62, 64
Robson, M. 61, 62, 64
Rodgers, J., 44, 45, 89, 91
Ruhleder, K. 29
Russell, T. 25, 50
Rutter, J. 21, 22, 48
Rybas, N. 10, 35, 36

Sade-Beck, L. 12
Sammons, P. 118
Sanders, T. 22, 40, 69, 94
Saunders, M. 53
Schneider, S.J. 24, 27
Schnettler, B. 6, 33, 40
Schwandt, T. 8, 9, 13
Selwyn, N. viii
Seymour, W. 11, 27, 32, 39, 76, 79, 108, 109
Sharf, B.F. 47, 61, 62, 63, 68, 83, 125
Shaw, R. 6
Sherr, L. 110, 111
Sikes, P. 58
Silverman, D. 12, 31, 111
Sixsmith, J. 48, 106
Slater, D. 35, 74, 75, 78, 81
Smith, A.D. 88
Smith, C. 39
Smith, G.W.H 21, 22, 48
Smith, R. 35
Spears, R. 20, 21
Sproull, L. 20, 32, 52
Stewart, F. 6, 11, 17, 21, 28, 33, 39, 48, 52,
   53, 59, 75, 77, 79, 80, 90, 106, 107, 111,
   115, 121, 131, 136
Stewart, K. 6, 23, 27, 28, 48, 107, 122, 135
Stone, A. 72
Stones, R. 11
Syniodinos, N. 32

Tanis, M. 20
Teli, M. 11, 13, 35
Thach, L. 32
Thorpe, R. 92
Thurlow, C. 109
Till, J.E. 68
Tomic, A. 109
Torres, C. 85
Treseder, P. 77
Trompenaars, F. 99
Tuffin, K. 9, 26, 29, 49, 62, 104, 106, 108,
   111, 113

Turkle, S. 9, 72, 73, 74, 78
Tusting, K. 105

Usher, R. 60

Vale, W. 86, 88, 122, 123
Van Mannen, J. 31
van Selm, M. 6, 89, 129
Vivari, B.J. 24, 27

Walford, G. 66, 67
Walker, K. 49, 62, 73, 76, 80, 110
Walstrom, M.K. 39
Walther, J.B. 62
Ward, K.J. 134
Warm, A. 119, 122, 123
Waskul, D. 62, 74, 81
Weber, M. 85
Wellens, J. 6
Wenger, E. 91, 99, 100

White, M. 47
Whitty, M.T. 54, 80, 101, 105
Williams, J.P. 47, 72, 97, 99, 101, 103, 104, 110
Williams, M. 6, 23, 27, 28, 47, 48, 107, 122, 135
Wilson, S.M. 77
Wittel, A. 32
Wolfreys, J. 44, 71, 74, 77, 139
Wood, C. 116, 117
Woolliams, P. 99
Wyn, E. 17

Xie, B. 77

Yearley, S. 112

Zhao, S. 5, 9, 44, 45, 49, 55, 74, 89, 101, 128
Zinkhan, G.E. 60
Zweerink, A. 22, 63, 75, 78

# Subject Index

# Supporting researchers for more than forty years

Research methods have always been at the core of SAGE's publishing. Sara Miller McCune founded SAGE in 1965 and soon after, she published SAGE's first methods book, *Public Policy Evaluation*. A few years later, she launched the Quantitative Applications in the Social Sciences series – affectionately known as the 'little green books'.

Always at the forefront of developing and supporting new approaches in methods, SAGE published early groundbreaking texts and journals in the fields of qualitative methods and evaluation.

Today, more than forty years and two million little green books later, SAGE continues to push the boundaries with a growing list of more than 1,200 research methods books, journals, and reference works across the social, behavioural, and health sciences.

From qualitative, quantitative and mixed methods to evaluation, SAGE is the essential resource for academics and practitioners looking for the latest in methods by leading scholars.

**www.sagepublications.com**

# SAGE Student Reference Guides

## Our bestselling books for undergraduates!

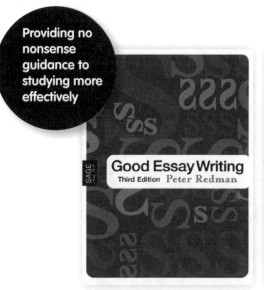

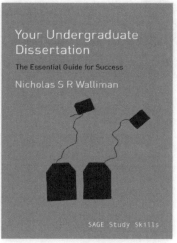

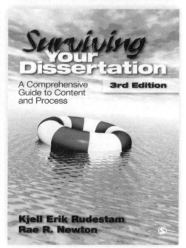

www.sagepub.co.uk/studyskills.sp

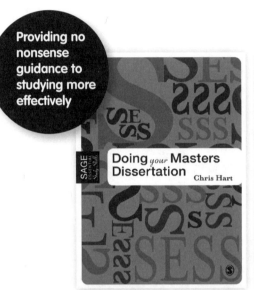
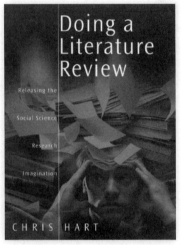
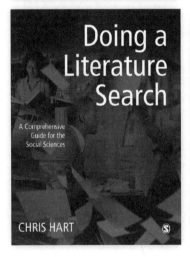